Brief Lives:
Gustave Flaubert

Brief Lives:
Gustave Flaubert

Andrew Brown

ET REMOTISSIMA PROPE

Brief Lives
Published by Hesperus Press Limited
4 Rickett Street, London sw6 1ru
www.hesperuspress.com

First published by Hesperus Press Limited, 2009

Copyright © Andrew Brown, 2009
The right of Andrew Brown to be identified as the Author of the Work
has been asserted by him in accordance with the Copyright, Designs
and Patents Act 1988.

Designed and typeset by Fraser Muggeridge studio
Printed in Jordan by Al-Khayyam Printing Press

isbn: 978-1-84391-902-5

Contents

The spire	9
The spiral	13
Vita brevis divi Gustavi	19
Childhood	27
School	33
Early writings	39
Élisa	45
Alfred Le Poittevin	49
Law	53
The sickness	57
Croisset	63
Maxime Du Camp	67
Deaths	73
Louise Colet	75
Louis Bouilhet	79
1848	83
Rejection	85
The East	89
Aesthetics at midnight	105
Madame Bovary	109
The trial	113
Paris life	119
Salammbô	123
Sentimental Education	133
1870–1	139
Saint Anthony	143
Ruin	147

Bouvard and Pécuchet   149
Three Tales   155
Influence   159

Bibliography   163
Acknowledgements   165
Biographical note   167

Life is brief and art is long
Flaubert, letter to Mlle Leroyer de Chantepie

Do not let us exchange 'tu quoque', as in a farce
Plato, *Phaedrus*, translated by Benjamin Jowett

The spire

The city of Rouen is dominated by its cathedral, and in particular by the black lattice-like structure rocketing up into the sky
from the nave, like a demented firework. Originally, in the
Middle Ages, a lantern tower had been designed; it was left
unfinished, and the stone spire meant to surmount it was never
built. A wooden spire, clad in lead, was added in 1540, but it burnt
down in 1822, months after Flaubert's birth. The architect Jean-
Antoine Alavoine (1778–1834) came up with a daring new design:
a spire, or rather *flèche*, made from prefabricated sections of cast
iron. Work was begun in 1824, but then proceeded very slowly;
interrupted in 1848, it was completed only in 1875, five years
before Flaubert's death. (In an open letter to the Rouen Town
Council in January 1872, he had suggested, bitingly, that they stop
blocking the plans for a commemorative bust of his friend and
fellow writer Louis Bouilhet and stick to matters that fell within
their field of competence – such as 'completing the sempiternal
flèche of the cathedral'.)

Alavoine was among the first wave of architects in France to
promote a return to the gothic style. His design for the *flèche* was
inspired by the delicately tapering spire of Salisbury Cathedral;
but his use of contemporary materials – an attempt to recreate
the spirit of the Middle Ages with that material of industrial
modernity *par excellence*, cast iron – was controversial. It was
criticised, for instance, by Alavoine's colleague Viollet-le-Duc,

who added the central *flèche* to Notre-Dame in Paris. Viollet-le-Duc viewed his own endeavours as both 'authentic' (in that they tried to capture the spirit of a bygone age), and 'creative' (adding elements that were imaginary, personal and contemporary) – and he freely admitted that he was often 'restoring' something that had never in fact existed. But he thought Alavoine's design was a compromise – a bit of a fake in its use of modern materials for a medieval structure.

As well as being a historical hybrid of dubious methodological integrity, the Rouen *flèche* can provoke very different reactions in visitors – Monet would later show how variously hued and grained the cathedral's great west façade can appear. Sometimes, especially at a distance, the *flèche* looks as if a slimline version of Blackpool Tower had been carefully lowered into position on top of the crumbling gothic pile; sometimes it looks almost extraterrestrially out of place, like a radio mast for communicating with other planets. Seen from below, it sizzles upwards, sputtering brilliant black sparks as it soars above the white stone pinnacles below: it both contradicts and continues the crockets and curlicues, the pediments and flying buttresses, of the ancient church. It simultaneously mimics and denies the past from which it springs. Some find it a powerful restatement of medieval themes; others find that it turns the cathedral into a jumble of composite elements that jar and clash. But even these admit that the mute ugliness of the whole can sometimes seem oddly expressive.

One visitor who was left quite cold by the *flèche* (admittedly uncompleted when he saw it) was the young lawyer Léon Dupuis. In *Madame Bovary* we read of how he has arranged to meet Emma at the cathedral. The amorous intent behind their rendezvous is unspoken, but powerfully skews their reaction to the monument of piety and art that looms above them. Inside the great cathedral, they are followed everywhere by an officious sacristan, anxious to share his knowledge with them; Léon tries to shake him off, and make his getaway to a more private place, with a still half-reluctant Emma in tow; but the worthy guide even follows them out into the street, imploring Léon at least to admire the *flèche*. 'No thanks,' says Léon, curtly, now desperate to hustle Emma into a cab. The sacristan simply cannot understand Léon's indifference, and continues to ply him with facts and figures. He has his monument, and insists on showing it off to all and sundry. He drones on, urgently, importunately. When the great *flèche* is finished, he tells his visitors proudly, 'it will be four hundred and forty feet high, nine less than the great pyramid of Egypt. It is made entirely of cast iron, it…' But Léon takes to his heels, with Emma tagging along; it seems to him that his love, which up until now has been as frozen as the stones in the church, is on the point of evaporating like smoke through 'that kind of truncated pipe, that oblong casing, that openwork chimney, which ventures so grotesquely above the cathedral like the crazy experiment of some fantastical metalworker'.

The restorative, historicising, medieval-style *flèche* still seems oddly, precariously, defiantly modern: gravity trying to heave itself into grace. Flaubert's work is sometimes acutely contemporary (*Madame Bovary*, *Sentimental Education*, *Bouvard and Pécuchet* are all set in nineteenth-century France, and the last two deal explicitly with the revolutionary events of the year 1848) and sometimes harks back to a remote past which it attempts to restore with extravagantly documented fidelity: *Salammbô* is set in third-century BC Carthage, *The Temptation of Saint Anthony* deals with the visions and spiritual struggles of a third to fourth century AD saint, the late short story 'Saint Julian Hospitator' is based on medieval hagiography, and 'Herodias' is set in the period just before the start of Christ's mission. The new stories show the persistence of the past on both collective and individual levels: Frédéric's devotion to Madame Arnoux, in *Sentimental Education*, is a replay of Mariolatry and courtly love at their most sublimated. Rather like Rouen Cathedral, Flaubert's work is situated between 'the waning of the Middle Ages' and the 'disenchantment of the world'. His writing reflects the political restlessness of nineteenth-century France: this was a country trying to modernise while constantly going round in circles. It also scrutinises the genesis of political and personal meanings. (One of the great pleasures of modern Flaubert scholarship is genetic criticism, which focuses on how, from the thousands of pages of drafts, he slowly and agonisingly groped towards the final form – how he got from *there* to *here*.) Flaubert is original because he is so very ancient, forever trying to discover the *origins* of the problem. Where does the novel, that most modern of literary genres, come from? In what ways does it render (or seem to render) lived experience intelligible, and at what price? In *Madame Bovary* he reinvents the novel; in some of his later works, *The Temptation of Saint Anthony* and 'Herodias', he grapples with the origins of a whole culture; and in his last, unfinished novel, *Bouvard and Pécuchet*, his inquisitive ex-copyist heroes speculate (comically, cosmically) on the origins of the entire universe. He is forever examining the ways in which human beings, from the mud of Normandy, the streets of Paris, or the sands of North Africa, in their 'crazy', experimental-conformist, ancient-and-modern ways, aspire.

The spiral

Flaubert's angle on contemporary events was unusually acute. 1848, the Springtime of Peoples, was a time on which Flaubert later looked back with considerable nostalgia ('the best year of my life', he wrote in 1878: yes, the best…); but this was not for any political reason, but because he had felt unusually full of youthful zest that year. It was also the year of a break-up – he split with his lover Louise Colet, temporarily – and of two deaths: his friend Alfred Le Poittevin, and his dog. These events were as important for him as the two revolutions that occurred in France that year. Likewise, he officially spent the years 1858–62 in the heyday of the Second Empire, but he was really in ancient Carthage. His life was governed not just by the untimeliness of anachronism, but by timelessness. As a young boy, he seemed so 'absent' from the world (gormless, open-mouthed, slow to talk and to read, generally out of it) that his parents were worried: maybe he was backward, especially as compared with his briskly efficient elder brother Achille? (From this parental anxiety, Sartre derived the title of his vast biographical study of Flaubert, *The Family Idiot*.) Flaubert himself spoke rather of his existence as being poor in events: it was 'flat and tranquil', and sentences were his only adventures. (It is ironic that, when he wrote this, he was just about to be put on trial for *Madame Bovary*; but this turned out to be a surprisingly positive affair as far as he was concerned.) 'What I do today I will do tomorrow, and I did the same yesterday. I was the same man ten years ago.' This was the eternal return of the same in the most everyday of senses: a routine adopted as a mask, the creation of an empirical self, with its identifiable quirks, that would get him from day to day while safeguarding what was most precious, lying too deep to be affected by surface events. He frequently spoke of the gap between inner and outer, and of the need to 'create for yourself, outside the existence that is visible, common and general to all, another internal existence, inaccessible to everything that falls within the domain of the contingent, as the philosophers say'.

His life was a mechanism with a regular rotation, and his narratives often seem to come full circle, or to close in on themselves. *Madame Bovary* begins and ends with an anonymous narrator who is (or pretends to be) absent the rest of the time; *Sentimental Education* closes with Deslauriers echoing, verbatim, Frédéric's concluding remark that a failed attempt to lose their virginity at a local brothel when they were boys had been 'the best time' they had known; 'Saint Julian' ends with Julian lying on top of a freezing leper to keep him warm, body against body, mouth against mouth. But all of these apparent images of repetition and closure are more complex than they seem. The Charles of the end of *Madame Bovary* is radically different from the diffident schoolboy we met at the beginning; admittedly, he is different largely because, after Emma's death, he has started to repeat some of her most characteristic gestures and attitudes – but this is precisely what constitutes his originality: a kind of crazy mimicry, an attempt to internalise her by copying her, the result of what the drafts to the novel note, several times over, is 'extreme love'. Deslauriers's repetition of Frédéric is not mere parroting; it may break one of Flaubert's cardinal rules (that it is stupid to conclude – not least because the two men are offering a premature judgement on lives that are not over), but it is an assent to Frédéric, a phatic of friendship. And Julian's embrace of the leper not only conflates, in the most extreme way imaginable, *eros* and *charis* (the leper's purulent sores have _why?_

been described in sickening detail), but is an act of closure (man mirroring man) and obedience to divine law that suddenly opens up a wholly new dimension.

If there is no pure repetition, there are variations on a basic theme, refrains that recur in new contexts. We seem to have gone round in a circle, but we end up in a place that is, though familiar, somewhere else. Flaubert was essentially a revisitor in his life and a rewriter in his work: this was how he made new things. He sometimes provoked events so that he could revisit them later, in memory (or, in heavily disguised form, in his writing). Indeed, much of his later career was spent, not so much imagining what he was going to write about, as researching it: somebody else needed to have been there first. The slowness with which he wrote (one word per hour, as the Goncourts' joke ran) was indeed stylistic, a matter of locating the right word, plotting the exact position of a semi-colon, timing the rhythm and cadence of a sentence; but it was also due to the acres of documentation through which he would plough, and the long hours of fieldwork in which he indulged. While composing _Bouvard and Pécuchet_, he wrote to his niece Caroline in September 1873 that he had travelled from Paris to Rambouillet by train, from Rambouillet to Houdan by calèche, from Houdan to Mantes by cabriolet, and back by train to Rouen, reaching Croisset at midnight, under a deluge of rain. The journey cost him eighty-three francs – 'a conscientious literature is expensive!' And all of these peregrinations were undertaken so that he could find a real house for his imaginary heroes Bouvard and Pécuchet to live in. (On this occasion he thought he _might_ have found a des res: but he wasn't quite sure, he still needed to check out the road between Chartres and Laigle...) He lived like a location scout: places were always potential settings. Even his quest for the '_mot juste_' implies a reality already out there, with only one proper way of describing it. He spoke of his fear of the empty page: his way of overcoming this fear was to blacken the page with ink, and then, once there was something there, correct it – like a painter with infinite *pentimenti*, or a manically interventionist copy editor of his own rough drafts. Then he could correct the corrections, reviewing, revising, revisiting. He produced one version of *Saint Anthony*: it met with a chilly reception. Instead of junking it, he returned to it twice over, producing two further, and very different, versions; and his choice of Saint Anthony as a subject matter emerged from the 'primordial soup' of youthful imaginings (stories of the Devil, of the world as a spectacle seen from a distance, of all the temptations of lust, power, and transcendence), jolted into a feasible and coherent fictional form by a painting of Saint Anthony probably by Jan Mandyn (Flaubert thought it was by one of the Breughels) that he saw while on holiday in Genoa. In 1845 he completed a novel called *Sentimental Education*; he never published it, and the novel of the same name that was given to the public in 1869 was different in almost every respect. The sombre theme of a woman's suicide is there in 'Passion and Virtue', written in 1837: from this, and other early stories, a complicated series of sheers, torques, and transformations led to *Madame Bovary* – and here again, the catalyst was possibly a nudge from the outside world, a friendly suggestion, a story in the papers. One of the very earliest pieces he wrote, a short satirical sketch on the beast known as a 'Clerk', returned, much revised and enlarged, at a later turn of the spiral, producing *Bouvard and Pécuchet*.

Flaubert was greatly influenced by one of his history teachers at school, Chéruel, who was later appointed to a chair in history at the *École normale supérieure*. Chéruel had been a pupil of the great Michelet, who had largely been responsible for introducing the thought of the Neapolitan Giambattista Vico into France. Vico's model of history takes the form of a spiral: various ages – the divine, the heroic, and the democratic – are followed by a period of chaos and then a *ricorso* to a new divine age, inaugurating another turn in the spiral. Flaubert's view of history became gradually simpler: by the time of the Franco-Prussian War, he had boiled it down to three stages: paganism, Christianity, boorishness. But the idea of the spiral lodged in his mind. It had a darker meaning than in Vico: there was no progress. The spiral was a demented fugue spinning off, from the 'trampoline' of reality, into imagination and ultimately madness. While he was laboriously digging his way into *Madame Bovary*, in 1852, he was constantly distracted by other temptations: by *Saint Anthony*, by the *Dictionary of Received Ideas* (a compendium of the clichés and stereotypes of conversation), but also by what he enigmatically called 'the uncertain sketch of a big metaphysical novel, fantastical and loudmouthed [*gueulard*]'. Its theme would be madness. Partly inspired by Dante's circles of hell, its protagonist would be a man who fostered his own hallucinations. A fragmentary sketch of this work, 'La Spirale', survives: it suggests how imaginary fulfilment is bought at the price of real dereliction. The unhappier the hero is in reality, the happier he is in his dreams. He restlessly changes jobs, becomes entangled in the world's toils (love, ambition, money), fails in all he undertakes. But every failure is projected into a grandiose image: an ordinary French *Préfet* (and to write a novel on the 'type' of this bastion of officialdom would be one of Flaubert's last projects) becomes 'a cruel and grotesque Sultan', the hero's beloved becomes an odalisque, a patrol of the National Guard is transformed into a huge army marching through the mountains – and the mere sight of a parish priest enables him to converse with Christ. 'He must be very naïve,' comments the draft. The 'spiral' would have comprised the various ordeals through which the hero was to pass; but the rather tentative conclusion was to be that 'happiness lies in imagination'. However, the sketch ends with the idea that the protagonist is to commit suicide, and the transfiguration of reality by Emma Bovary and Flaubert's other dreamers, and maybe by Flaubert himself, exacts its sacrifice.

Flaubert's life, as well as his work, was lived under the sign of the spiral: it was a matter of many returns, not always happy (or even unhappy). In Marseille, on the way back from a holiday in Corsica, in 1840, he was seduced by the exotic, sonorously named Eulalie Foucaud Delanglade, a thirty-five-year-old Creole; typically, he had just been swimming, and she was aroused by this healthy, handsome young man with wet hair. After their brief but passionate encounter, he left for Normandy; there were tears on their separation, and then letters (she wrote that their souls were now married). He returned to Marseille five years later, intending to see her again: before going, he told his friend Alfred Le Poittevin that he expected to find that she was now ugly – not that disillusionment was anything other than *poetic*. But whether or not her looks had faded as she hit *la quarantaine*, he was never to know, for she wasn't there: the hotel was abandoned, the shutters closed. Each time he went back to Marseille (including just before he set sail for Egypt), she was absent; each time, her absence was different, at another turn of the spiral. On his way to do fieldwork for *Salammbô* in April 1858, he stopped by again. It was now a decade since *la belle tétonnière* had given him such a sweet welcome; but the ground floor of the hotel was now occupied by a toy shop, and the first floor was a barber's, which he visited twice, for a philosophical shave, while trying (in vain) not to indulge in Chateaubriandesque reflections on passing days, falling leaves – and thinning hair. He wandered around for two days, feeling lonely, and sitting amid the sailors in out-of-the-way cafés, gazing at the sea. 'The circle has shrunk. The thoughts that passed through my mind in 1849, when I embarked for Egypt, will pass through it again in a few days as I walk the same streets.' Spirals could contract as well as expand.

Vita brevis divi Gustavi

Sometimes Flaubert thought you could never be too brief about his life. It can be summed up in a single sentence. Gustave Flaubert was a doctor's son who devoted his bachelor existence to becoming a master of French prose and exploring every degree of human folly and stupidity. Or, even more accurately, as:

... in other words, a blank – like the one in *Sentimental Education* between the coup d'état of December 1851 and Frédéric's return from his elliptically noted travels abroad. Brief life? *What* life...? He had no biography, he claimed: typical writer's *coquetterie*, often copied since (*vide* Beckett, Dürrenmatt, Anouilh, et al), but, in his case, with a particularly Flaubertian edge of pride and defensiveness. There was just the writing – and yet the negative capability of being an author could be burdensome. 'Oh how much money I'd give to be either more stupid or more clever, an atheist or a mystic, but at least something complete, entire, an identity, in a word, something.' He was a one-man factory for producing fictions: the title of the art review *L'Art industriel* that Jacques Arnoux runs in *Sentimental Education* may purport to convey an oxymoron, but it can be applied with satisfying aptness to Flaubert, even if he himself would have preferred more craftsmanlike metaphors: the manual labour of writing, the almost assembly-belt repetitiveness of technique, the finicky adjustments (inserting a comma here, loosening a paragraph transition there) of the whole procedure, the back-breaking hours at his desk, and the roundedness of the sentences that emerged from the hours of polishing, are reminiscent of the tax-collector Binet in *Madame Bovary*, who spends his leisure hours turning round napkin rings on a lathe whose buzz drifts across the roofs of Yonville. Like Binet, the author doesn't have a life, he has a lathe. Flaubert called himself an 'Homme-plume', a Quill-man, or (like Shem in *Finnegans Wake*) a Penman (most of his friends would be, essentially, Penfriends): life was merely an ellipsis that interrupted the process of blackening the pages. Unless he was either reading, writing, or thinking about reading and writing, he suspected he might well go mad. The quill (he was old-fashioned enough to prefer a goose quill to its more modern, iron version) was his prosthesis: scalpel, tentacle, antenna, proboscis – as well as standing in, at times, for more obvious organs.

Even the No-life Quill-man was capable, in 1846, of jokily dreaming about 'paying people to write my biography as one of the great men of the present day'. And he toyed with the genre of autobiography. On 18th March 1857, when he was *nel mezzo*, etc., he wrote to one of his correspondents, Mlle Leroyer de Chantepie, giving her his own 'complete portrait and biography': 'I'm thirty-five years old, five foot eight inches high, I have the shoulders of a stevedore and the nervous irritability of a *petite maîtresse*. I am a bachelor and live alone.' (He actually stood over six feet tall – feet and thumbs were different in France.) But this laconic self-blurb comes after rather a lot of incidental information: he had been a pilgrim in the Holy Land; he had got lost in the snows of Parnassus ('which can be seen as symbolic'); and his dream was to move into a little *palazzo* on the Grand Canal in Venice (a dream not far removed from those of several of his characters).

The writer Ernest Feydeau was aware of the value of a little self-advertising; he urged Flaubert to indulge in this potentially remunerative activity, and in 1859 tried to persuade him to give some details to a biographer for an article. Flaubert replied:

'As for my anonymous biographer, what do you want me to send him as a favour? I have no biography. Tell him whatever you want – make it up if necessary' (an invitation that it would be churlish to decline). But this indulgent tone soon gives way to something more splenetic. The moustache bristles, the eyes bulge, the face darkens. The minute you're an artist, Flaubert growls, *messieurs* the grocers, the inspectors, the customs officials, the bootmakers *en chambre* and others all start enjoying themselves at your expense! There are people to tell them whether you're blond or dark-haired, facetious or melancholy, how old you are, and 'whether you're inclined to drink or to playing the harmonica'. (For the sake of *messieurs* the grocers, etc., the answers to these questions are: blond, but *prematurely* bald; both, fiercely; thirty-seven at the time of the letter; occasionally, for instance at the Magny dinners; probably not to concert-performing level.) 'I think, on the contrary, that the writer must never leave anything of himself behind but his works. His life is of little importance. Back off, old man! [*Arrière, la guenille!*]'

… Whereupon, in the same letter to Feydeau, he invents a nice little biographical sketch of himself, Rabelaisian in tone. He has uttered all the most famous quotations in history, he asserts; he was a handsome little boy, and his nursemaids wanked him off with such vigour that they dislocated their shoulders; he knew oriental languages before he was ten; he saved forty-eight people from fires; he wore out all the women in the Grand Turk's harem; he slew thirty cavalrymen in a duel; – and publishers fought to get his manuscripts.

In his last decade, he composed a more unctuous mock-biography of one of his alter egos – a portrait of the artist as an old Jesuit by the name of the 'Reverend Father Cruchard', dedicated to George Sand's granddaughter Aurore Dupin. He told of how he had been born in a cider press in the diocese of Lisieux and how, as a young boy, he had tended the flocks in the fields, singing canticles and sculpting objects of piety out of wood. His devoutness was noted, and he was admitted to study at the seminary at Lisieux. Here, Cruchard was extremely hard-working – but always bottom of the class. Indeed, he appeared quite stupid. But a pilgrimage improved his intelligence, and soon he was a scholastic star. He wrote a Latin tragedy on *The Destruction of Sodom* – a scabrous subject that he treated with such allusive discretion that nobody could tell what on earth it was about: still, suspicions remained, and it was never performed. He turned instead to the study of logic, to the great Aquinas: as a preacher, the fervour of his delivery (he 'thundered forth' in his sonorous voice) swelled the congregation. Exhausted by his oratorical labours, he travelled to Italy to drink at the fountain of the arts – 'he studies, he annotates, he devours everything!' He returned to compose learned treatises, including a three-volume folio work on the Tower of Babel. Summoned to the royal court at Versailles, he soon became a favoured spiritual director for the ladies, who flocked to hear the words of wisdom that dropped from his mellifluous lips.

There's many a true word: the bantering, wheedling tone of these little *jeux d'esprit* cannot disguise the fact that Flaubert, who often spoke of himself as a priest wedded to his art (or a mad monk, or a hermit with an itchy hair-shirt) is here giving us a made-over version of his life: his fascination for quoting (or mimicking quotation), his apparent backwardness as a boy, his literary endeavours whose mixture of aesthetic guardedness and *risqué* subject-matter creates such unease, the travels, the erudition, the way he could act as a kindly and wise advisor to so many ladies (albeit generally on the epistolary level)… He may even be representing, at one remove, his own life as a confidant of Princess Mathilde Bonaparte in the courts of the Second Empire.

Flaubert, of course, insisted on the gap between his life and his art. 'Hide your life', he urged on a correspondent (quoting Epicurus). And: 'The artist must take care that posterity will think he never lived.' He was, in this respect, disastrously careless: materials for his biography lie scattered like piles of detritus at the foot of the Pyramids. Thanks to this, and to Flaubert's indulgence in blokish sexual banter with such friends as Louis Bouilhet, we know exactly how many orgasms he enjoyed with the Egyptian courtesan Kuchuk Hanem, and their varying quality, from 'fierce' (no. 3), to 'sentimental' (no. 5, the last). He did joke that he would like to be buried with his manuscripts, in the way savages were buried with their horses – 'after all, it's those poor dear pages that have helped me cross the long plain'. *Flaubertiana* would then be a matter of archaeology. But a big pit would have been needed to contain all the paper – and as it was, the hole dug in the Rouen cemetery for his coffin was too small, as the gravediggers discovered with some embarrassment at his funeral. (Some of the mourners, who had been reminiscing about the funeral of Emma Bovary, now reflected on the hardness of the Norman earth; others remembered a similar poignant misadventure at the funeral of Flaubert's sister Caroline; and others thought of vague immensities or wondered at what point it would not be deemed too impolite to smoke.)

As well as the manuscripts, there are the letters. They were André Gide's bedtime reading, an endless source of energy to be tapped into – they even replaced his Bible. Thanks to them, Flaubert, the most avowedly impersonal of writers, has the strongest (or at least loudest) personality of any nineteenth-century French author. But Flaubert's secret, even if his *opus* is extended to include his drafts, letters, and laundry bills, may still be safe. Freud once looked at the serried volumes of Goethe's collected works and said, 'To think that he wrote all that in order to conceal himself' (even from Freud). As Flaubert told one correspondent, 'It's by working that I manage to silence my innate melancholy.' But 'the old depths that nobody knows, the deep wound that remains hidden' was there in the silence.

In any case, we know of his hostility to people taking an interest in his life only because of people taking an interest in his life.

Sartre's *The Family Idiot* draws on Marxism and existentialist psychoanalysis to explain the tiniest details of Flaubert's life and work and show that 'artist' was as much of a determinate position as all the others. Like Bourdieu's later *The Rule of Art*, it both attempts to situate Flaubert in his time, and to explore the limits (if any) of such a situating. Sartre takes seriously Flaubert's elevation of art to an Idea; he knows that, in some senses, in taking on (in tackling) Flaubert, he is taking on Literature: for Flaubert *is* literature, its most strident and authoritative representative, hallowed by his long passion and martyrdom. The blood of the martyrs is the seed of the Church: Flaubert was the martyr of his own deity, literature, and he daily shed his ink in its service. But Sartre also knows that he is taking on 'Flaubert = Literature' in another way; in his own word, *assuming* it, and, even when he is critically dismantling it, endorsing it. By attempting to trace the choices and stratagems that led Flaubert to make of literature an Idea, Sartre is also making his own contribution to the disenchantment of literature, bringing it down from the heavens to the earth. But Flaubert had already done so, and demonstrated that literature is its own disenchantment. So Sartre sometimes claimed that *The Family Idiot* was both an attack on the Flaubertian novel, with its air of impassivity and autonomy, and itself a novel that happened to be true. He refused to alter the facts in the life of his subject (this would have been tantamount to depriving him, posthumously, of his liberty); but he used his own novelistic imagination to fill in the inevitable gaps in the account. In this way, and deploying a sumptuous vocabulary (Gustave's fatness is symptomatic of the 'facticity of the flesh' – this may sound funny, but that does not make it untrue: *au contraire*), Sartre remorselessly tracked down his *frère ennemi*, his double, the one who had suffered from (and to some extent created) the same *mal littéraire* as Sartre himself.

The Family Idiot is thus one 'brief life' of Flaubert. 'Brief' because even the 2,700 pages we have are incomplete, and we have still not reached *Madame Bovary*; Sartre's near-blindness forestalled any *finis*, but he had in fact covered much of his subject's existence since, as many writers on Flaubert have observed, starting with Flaubert himself, Flaubert was more or less done – finished, or perhaps stuck – at a very early age. This may be true of everybody – but it is even truer of Flaubert. Almost every writer complains about the pain of writing; so did Flaubert, but more so. The idea that Flaubert was in a sense deeply ordinary, only more so, and that this was one of the reasons for his magnificent anger, was put about by the Goncourt brothers, in their diary: it has a certain plausibility. He attempted to conceal his commonness, they thought, by 'truculent paradoxes, depopulating axioms, revolutionary bellowings, a brutal and indeed ill-brought-up way of setting himself against all received and accepted ideas'.

But Flaubert at an early age was a distinctly singular creature.

Childhood

The blood that ran through his veins was Norman blood, vineg-
ary, like cider: so he sometimes wrote (ignoring the more obvious
fact that the fluid his heart really pumped round his imposing
frame was ink). He was sometimes compared to a blond Viking
warrior: and everything suggests (especially the magnificent
moustache and the increasingly prominent paunch) that this
obelisk of French literature also looked a little like Obelix.

He admitted, reluctantly, that his ancestors had in all reality
probably been quite decent folk; never mind that; he would
rewrite the facts to suit his royal, or roguish, fantasy; he was
composed of 'Tartar, Scythian, Bedouin, Redskin' elements – and
'there's some monk in there' (a monk who had clearly, to be part
of Flaubert's bloodline, broken his vows). These fantasies often
took concrete shape: he took time off from writing *Madame
Bovary* to attend a fancy-dress party at Madame Sabatier's Paris
salon, dressed as a Red Indian warrior, waving a kitchen sieve
around as a tomahawk. No casualties were reported. (The year
before Flaubert died, Edmond de Goncourt noted his 'brick-red'
countenance; with the wisp of hair on his bare cranium, he
looked like a cross between a Jordaens painting and a North
American Indian.) He wished to identify with all savages, all
outsiders.

He resented the fact that he had been born in Rouen ('the city
has fine churches and stupid inhabitants, I loathe it, I hate it'):

he sometimes even denied it – his eyes had opened on altogether other skies. He had always existed. (Life? Been there. Done that. Everything is anamnesis; everything is the rewriting of a pre-existent script.) His memories went back to the Pharaohs. 'I can see myself at different historical periods, quite clearly, carrying out different trades, with many different degrees of success. My present self is the result of my vanished selves. – I was a boatman on the Nile, a *leno* [pimp] in Rome at the time of the Punic Wars, then a Greek *rhetor* in Subura, where I was eaten up by the fleas. – I died during the Crusades after eating too many grapes on the shores of Syria. I've been a pirate and a monk, a mountebank and a coach-driver. Perhaps Emperor of the East too?' So he wrote at the age of forty-one, when most people have long since forgotten their previous lives. He remembered his time in Subura with particular intensity. This poor, overcrowded quarter of ancient Rome was plague-ridden and prone to fire; Juvenal derided Hannibal for having wished to plant his banner in such a sordid corner of the great capital. But the aristocrat Julius Caesar had been born here, and the coexistence of high and low life made it an eminently Flaubertian place. In the middle of the nineteenth century, with its steam ships, its factories, and its train timetables ('modern stupidity and grandeur are symbolised by a railway' – an unusually balanced appraisal, for Flaubert), he longed to elbow his way through the thronged streets of Subura when the torches burned at the brothel doors… And when he did actually, in his current incarnation, travel to Rome, he told his friend Louis Bouilhet (whose long poem *Melaenis* was set partly in Subura) that he would pay a special visit to that most enticing of districts. (Perhaps all his previous lives were – literature?) Travelling through Greece, he remembered that he had already wandered across it – he had been, 'under the Roman Empire, the manager of some group of travelling players, one of those fellows who went off to Sicily in search of women to turn into actresses – men who were teachers, pimps and artists all at the same time'. His historical reveries were often linked to women: to prostitutes and actresses in particular. If he was alive to the allure of the streetwalkers, in their low-cut dresses, coming out to ply their trade at dusk in Rouen or Paris, it was because they made him think of antiquity, for the oldest profession straddled every age of masculine lust – and he was unsurprised to find erotic paintings on the walls of Egyptian tombs. The study of history was a morose delectation, a sombre form of Eros. 'As if our own past were not enough for us, we chew over the past of the whole of humanity and we delight in that voluptuous bitterness.'

When he did describe himself to others, in his letters, he resorted either to facetious evasion or to metaphor. In this latter respect he is close to the symbolist poets of the latter part of the nineteenth century: Baudelaire's 'I am like the king of a rain-sodden land' or Verlaine's 'I am the Empire at the end of the age of decadence', both sentiments which Flaubert could have shared, though his objective identifications were often rather less grandiose. He was an assemblage of disparate elements, an 'arabesque in marquetry', made of pieces of ivory, gold and iron, of painted cardboard and diamond and tinplate. He was a traveller's trunk, where everything was neatly in its place, compartmentalised away into different drawers, all tied up and lashed down. Sometimes he was more amorphous: a lake, or 'a stagnant pool where nothing moves and nothing can be seen'. As he feared passion and movement, this was a good thing, for 'if happiness is to be found anywhere, it's in stagnation. Ponds never suffer from storms.' Shortly before his death, he liquefied like an old camembert. Above all, of course, he was a whole bestiary: a tiger (with 'a sharp prick that wounds others, and myself too, sometimes'), a horse (knackered), a dromedary (difficult to start, difficult to stop). He wanted to be a leopard he saw in a painting in Naples; but usually he was a gross, plodding creature, something 'colossal, monumental' – an ox, a sphinx, a bittern, an elephant, 'everything that's most enormous, bloated and heavy, psychologically as well as physically'. He wrote this in July 1841, at an age when the world still saw him as an alert, tall, slender teenager: but no, in his own eyes, he was very like a whale. He marinaded like an oyster in a jar, he warmed himself in the bright sun of beauty like 'a literary lizard', he was a dreamy, fearful hare, living in leaps and bounds – but most of all, he was a bear, especially a polar bear, digging a deep hole in which he could maintain a constant temperature, and staying there. 'The Aïnos [Ainu],' he once noted, 'an indigenous tribe of Yezo, an island in the north of Japan, worship the Bear as god. When they have hunted one and killed it, they dissect it with great ceremony and address many a genuflexion and prayer to the deceased deity.' One of the most grouchily diligent of all bear hunters is Geoffrey Braithwaite, in Julian Barnes's *Flaubert's Parrot*. Braithwaite's wanderings interact with an exploded, disseminated biography of a Flaubert in permanent eruption (firing off misanthropic missives packed with a wonderfully quotable querulousness); the tragic facetiousness of Braithwaite's tone (his wife's life was cut short by madness and suicide) make his book a 'true novel', like Sartre's, and the best brief life of Flaubert imaginable.

For Flaubert, these flight-lines into other animate or inanimate existences were all attempts to escape from society, which not only forced him to be one thing but made him one of a herd. All of his animals (flying somewhat against the zoological facts) are solitary. 'I don't want to be part of anything, to belong to any academy, any corporation, any association whatsoever. I hate the herd, the rule and the norm. A Bedouin, yes, as much as you like; a citizen, never.' There would be times when a strange feeling of solidarity did override this aloofness, in particular during the Franco-Prussian War, when he became the most patriotic of Frenchmen and was happy, as a member of the National Guard, to drill his men up and down the banks of the Seine. But on the whole, animals were better – and sometimes even that was asking too much. 'Action has always disgusted me to the highest degree. It seems to belong to the animal side of existence.' So he'd rather really be a meditative, intellectual 'mushroom', or spend the next thirty years stuffed with hashish (if he weren't so nervous of taking it), lying inert on his back, 'like a log'.

This comatose amoeba, with its pseudopods stretching out across space and time, was also a child. 'I was born in the hospital (of Rouen – my father was chief surgeon there; he has left a name that is illustrious in his art), and I grew up in the midst of every human wretchedness – from which I was separated by a wall.' Gustave lived in the top storey of the three-floor Hôtel-Dieu (then the main hospital in Rouen): his imagination was soon crossing the 'wall', especially in the 1832 cholera epidemic – he later remembered that the family dining room was separated from a sick ward where people were 'dropping like flies'. Brief lives. (The 'Museum of Flaubert and the History of Medicine' – a significant 'and' – occupies part of the old Hôtel-Dieu, and includes a section on infant mortality, as well as the skull of one of Gustave's literary heroes, Sade.) His father, Achille-Cléophas, was strong-willed, energetic, a freemason and political liberal. He had been a pupil of the great Dupuytren, famous for his contracture (discovered in 1831). As an apprentice at the Anatomy and Physiology school in Rouen, Achille-Cléophas assisted Laumonier in the making of anatomical wax figures. His mother, Justine-Caroline, seems to have been emotionally chilly and yet over-protective towards her children, prone to headaches and other nervous ailments: early bereavement would increase her fragility and hypochondria.

The garden in which Gustave and his younger sister Caroline played was overlooked by the operating theatre, and he remembered climbing up the trellis with her and 'hanging amid the vines, peering curiously at the exposed cadavers! The sun was shining down on them; the same flies that darted over us and the flowers would go and settle on them, and come back, buzzing! […] I can still see my father lifting his head up from his dissection and telling us to go away.' In 1869, some years after *Madame Bovary* had been published, a now famous caricature of Flaubert by Lemot showed him wielding a scalpel on which the heart of his heroine was impaled. (Perhaps the scalpel was *le mot juste*.) Gustave claimed that he had even played in the operating theatre – 'that is why, perhaps, I come across as both morbid and cynical. I don't love life and I'm not afraid of death.' For him, the Lautréamont-esque meeting of an umbrella and a sewing machine on an operating table would have seemed rather tame.

He also claimed (in the same letter to Louise Colet) that, when he was still just a boy of six, his uncle, François Parain, had led him through Rouen's backstreets, which swarmed with prostitutes, and taken him to the *Hospice général* where, in the cells, he saw 'sitting and bound round the middle of their bodies, naked to their waists and completely dishevelled, a dozen or so women howling and scratching at their faces with their fingers. In those days I was maybe six or seven years old. They are good impressions to have when you're young; they make a man of you.'

So Gustave grew up, in a comfortable, bourgeois household where the madhouse, the brothel, and the morgue were never very far away. The world pressed in on him, with its corpses and its buzzing flies; he would gaze at it, mouth agape, or go off into one of the trances that worried his parents.

School

At the Collège Royal de Rouen, which he entered as a boarder in March 1832, aged ten, he was given a good grounding in the classics, came top of his class five times, studied maps of antiquity, and learned to compose sonorous orations in a dead language. He also spent a lot of time in the latrines. Years later, he took a brief holiday from his immersion in the vanished world of *Salammbô* and revisited his old school. He was indignant to see that the two yards for senior and junior boys respectively had now been completely segregated: no more fraternal smugging. The old latrines, with their deep puddles of urine and the cubicles in which he and his school friends had retired for a smoke, and 'wanked off so poetically between chilblain-ravaged fingers', were gone. (His imagination was often excrementitious, and he drew inspiration from images of the shit on which the palaces of culture were built. When the cesspool-men went on strike, in the mid-1860s, he did not think of agitating in favour of an improvement in their working conditions, but instead contemplated writing an ode.)

The strict, military-religious discipline of school life (though the food was always wholesome and copious) was also relieved by a glimpse of the private vices behind the public virtues. He was delighted to inform Ernest Chevalier, in March 1837, that the *censeur d'études* M. C***, who had 'a dirty shirt, dirty stockings, a dirty soul' and was, in short, 'a swine', had been caught in a brothel and was going to be hauled up before the academic council. 'What larks [*voilà qui est une bonne blague*]!' The young Gustave couldn't help thinking of the expression on the *censeur*'s face when rudely interrupted while he was 'getting his end away': it made him cry out, laugh, drink, sing, bang on the table, pull out his hair, roll on the ground – and utter the laugh of 'the Boy'.

'The Boy' (*Le Garçon*) was an invention of Gustave and his friends Ernest Chevalier and Alfred Le Poittevin, and his fictional deeds and sayings enlivened their meetings and correspondence for years. He was an odd character, both conformist and anarchist, a spouter of clichés (which his creators mimicked: passing Rouen Cathedral, they would declaim: 'this Gothic architecture – so beautiful, so uplifting!') and a wildly irreverent enactor of obscene celebrations (inviting his guests to a *'Fête de la merde'* at the Hôtel des Farces: buckets of shit and wooden dildos would be provided). He was, like Jarry's Père Ubu, like many members of that self-conscious class the bourgeoisie, like Gustave Flaubert himself, both bourgeois and *bourgeoisophobus*.

It was still an age of revolutionary and romantic fervour. One senior pupil composed an 'Apology for Robespierre', another wore a red bonnet, another wanted to go and fight with the forces of Abd-al-Qadir, the national hero of the Algerians in their struggle against the French; the intellectual atmosphere was 'troubadour, insurrectional and oriental – above all, artistic', Flaubert later remembered; there was a wave of suicides, inspired, not by Goethe's *Werther*, but by Dumas's *Antony*; one pupil shot himself, another hanged himself with his cravat; everyone admired Victor Hugo.

Gustave's good marks at school had soon reassured his parents that he was not, after all, a total idiot. The culture he absorbed was in many respects declamatory. Cicero's forensic and political speeches, and Bossuet's sermons, alerted him to the power of ornate, written language when it was given voice. This might have led him to the theatre (this was the great age of the romantic *tirade*); but his official ventures in that respect failed. An odd little satirical play on politics, called *The Candidate*, was taken off in 1874, after only four performances: a fiasco comparable to Henry James's *Guy Domville*, though less traumatic for the thicker-skinned Flaubert, who simply joined the band of dramatists whose works had flopped onstage, and who came together to have dinner regularly. They included Turgenev: his fellow writers were surprised to hear him claim earnestly that he had indeed been booed in Russia, but Russia was too far away for any of them to go and check. A Flaubertian *féerie*, a kind of staged fairytale, called *The Castle of Hearts* was another late venture, to whose *mise en scène* Flaubert devoted almost Wagnerian care: it was submitted to several theatre managers, but turned down. The three versions of *Saint Anthony* are all set out as dramas, with stage directions, set speeches, and indications of a (fantastical) setting – but they were never really meant to be performed (though theatrical productions have often been a great success: Béjart produced it as a ballet, described approvingly by one critic as a 'baroque and Freudian *diablerie*'). But the dramatist in Flaubert had in any case chosen prose for his theatre of operations – not because his prose was dramatic (far from it), but because it was in a sense to be declaimed. From *Madame Bovary* onwards, he would test out all of his prose fiction by reading it aloud – often by bellowing it at the top of his voice, either as he walked up and down in the garden at Croisset, or in the solitude of his study (from where he could still be heard outside, even with the windows closed). Only this way of performing the text, assaying the writing by performing it as speech (or as sustained yell), would enable him to eliminate undesirable assonances and eradicate the harsh grinding of consonantal clusters. He frequently complained that he had difficulty writing conversation – how could his characters speak in a way that was both as inconsequential as ordinary speech, and yet formally beautiful? But in some respects this was a pseudo-problem: the whole text was a speech. And this is the best way to read Flaubert: by belting it out. Create a real hoohah. Uproar in class! 'NOUS ÉTIONS A L'ÉTUDE, LORSQUE LE PROVISEUR ENTRA...' You can try it out on translations too, and judge whether they catch the authentic yell of the original: translation has always greeted howlers with open arms. Kafka, in his diary, 16th March 1912: 'Read Flaubert aloud with satisfaction.' Literature: for crying out loud.

Like everyone else, Gustave was punished by being given lines. Charles Bovary, whose first day at his new school is attended by a mild bout of ragging among the boys, is made to copy out *Ridiculus sum*, that *cogito* of Flaubert's world. Flaubert himself – whose last novel ends with two copyists copying out anything and everything – would later express his gratitude towards this unenlightened pedagogy, which at least meant that, when rereading the *Aeneid*, he could greet Virgil as an old friend.

He worked his way reluctantly through Mallet's *Manuel de philosophie*, the school textbook, but much preferred Montaigne, who wrote essays on such subjects as 'Sadness', on 'How the soul discharges its emotions against false objects when lacking real ones', on 'How the taste of good and evil things depends in large part on the opinion we have of them', on 'The power of the imagination', on the fact that 'It is madness to judge the true and the false from our own capacities', on 'The uncertainty of our judgement', on 'The vanity of words', and 'On books'. Gustave studied Seneca, who wrote *otium sine litteris mors est* (leisure minus literature equals death), but in secret read Sade. (He later called Sade 'the last word in Catholicism' and 'the spirit of the medieval church'.) He studied Cicero, and later quoted (like another Gustave, or Gustav – von Aschenbach) his dictum on the *motus animi perpetuus* of eloquence, but he read the exuberantly scatological and encyclopaedically learned Rabelais. He won several prizes – for history, and for natural history. Little French literature was studied (literature was almost entirely an extra-curricular affair). Still, Flaubert did well in French composition. But then he was expelled.

He and other students had protested against what they saw as an unjust *pensum* imposed on a class by a teacher with discipline problems. This Latin word was the term applied to extra work given as a punishment. (It originally referred to the weight of wool that had to be handed over as part of a daily task, and it has the same etymology as the word 'pensive'. A Joycean pun can be extracted from it and applied to Flaubert, not to mention Joyce: *pen-sum*.) For various reasons (including Flaubert's daringly taking a stand on what he saw as a point of principle), Gustave, and two classmates who had 'refused the *pensum*', were told they would not be able to continue their studies. Although embarrassing for his parents, this was not a great disaster: he could still prepare for his baccalaureate alone, as what the French call a *cavalier seul*. This was hard work: he wrote to Chevalier telling him that he was studying from 3 a.m. to 8.30 p.m.; he smoked so much to see him through this ordeal that he would have been able to sit for his *tobaccalaureate*. In his *Dictionary of Received Ideas*, the *bac* is one of the things that all right-minded people 'thunder against'. So much studying, imposed on someone whose agenda had been set long ago, and who was soon feeling stifled. (About this time, he wrote in a notebook, 'I am a mute who wants to speak.') But he passed his *bac*, and grew a blond moustache.

Maybe he never really left the school that had expelled him. The notion of the *pensum* hovers like a glowering taskmaster over his writing. A century later, in the *Encyclopedia acephalica*, Michel Leiris would view such slavishness with disdain: being a good surrealist, he affected to look down on alienated labour. 'Leaving aside children who set fire to haystacks, derail trains or dream up great massacres of animals, I know scarcely any but sinister pedants who, chewing on their pen holders, sweat blood and water so as to write out to the bitter end their calamitous *pensums*…' It was life itself that sometimes struck Flaubert as a *pensum*: he was tired of getting up, putting on his clothes, eating. The opinions that constituted one of the great pleasures of bourgeois life were a burden to him, and having to have an opinion about anything at all was torment. 'I am as void of opinions as it is possible to be; objections for and against seem to me equally valid. I'd decide on a heads or tails basis and not regret the outcome, whatever it might be' – this he wrote in a letter to Du Camp on 21st October 1851. To every opinion there was an equally valid counter-opinion (though there was also, unfortunately, a counter-opinion to this statement too). He added that, if he did ever publish *Saint Anthony*, it would be 'in the most stupid way possible [*le plus bêtement du monde*]. Because I've been told to do it, out of imitation, out of obedience and without any initiative on my part' – a pure *pensum*, as was *Madame Bovary*. It was as if, long after he had successively passed his baccalaureate, he had actually (for what infraction of the rules?) been kept behind at school, writing out his lines in solitude when all the other boys had long since departed.

And yet, for many years he had already been writing – and not out of duty, not as a school exercise: for no reason at all other than sheer *joie d'écrire*, with all the fraught pleasures that this entailed.

Early writings

He had been late in learning to read. Why bother, when there were always others to tell you stories, and read to you out of strange boxes full of fluttering bits of paper with black signs on them? His nursemaid Julie told him about ghosts and goblins; an elderly neighbour known as Père Mignot read him *Don Quixote* in a children's version, which Gustave (who had a very retentive memory) soon knew off by heart. He would become so absorbed in his reading – twisting a lock of his hair in his fingers and biting his tongue – that on one occasion he fell off his chair flat on the floor; another time, he collided with the glass of some book-shelves and cut his nose.

Almost as soon as he had learned his letters, he was writing them. As would so often later be the case (any bit of the correspondence you quote can be put down by another), we, who can compare what he wrote to different addressees, can see how he changed epistolary persona. One of the first datable letters he wrote, to his grandmother, on 1st January 1830 (he was nine years old), wished her a Happy New Year; to his friend Ernest Chevalier, a year later, he wrote: 'You're right to say that New Year's Day is stupid.' And he continued: 'If you like we can get together I'll write plays and you'll write your dreams and as there's a lady who comes to see papa and who always talks nonsense to us [*qui nous contes* [sic] *toujours de bêtises*] I'll write them.' So it began: a lifetime of writing down *bêtises*: of writing (about) stupidity.

A few years later, on 14th August 1835, again to Ernest, he gets political, only to decide that his mind is ultimately fixed on higher things: 'I am indignant to see that censorship of the stage is going to be re-established and freedom of the press abolished; yes, this law will go through because the representatives of the people are nothing but a bunch of traitors [*vendus*], their aims are mere self-interest, their inclination is towards servility, their honour is a stupid arrogance, their souls are a dung-hill, but one day, a day that will come soon, the people will begin the third revolution [...] Farewell, so long, and let us always concentrate on art, which, greater than all peoples, crowns and kings is always there, hanging aloft, borne up by enthusiasm, taking its diadem from God.' Other letters to Ernest end with 'kiss my arse'; or complain 'Your opinions on V. Hugo are quite true, and quite unoriginal [*peu tiennes*]'; or they philosophise: 'I have come to the point where I look upon the world as a spectacle, and laugh at it.'

As well as the letters, there was also 'art': a eulogy on Corneille (who had been born in Rouen), and a 'Grand Explanation of The Celebrated Constipation', which focuses on the *trou merdarum* (turdicous hole) and its dysfunctions. Corneille is praised for producing 'flawless' works; the hole is berated for its failure to produce anything much. At this logorrhoeal stage, constipation still seemed like a joke.

In 1831, at the age of ten, he completed a summary of the reign of Louis XIII and dedicated it to his mother. Between then and 1845, when he finished the first version of *Sentimental Education*, he composed over forty titles. The themes of the first are often historical: stories about 'The Plague in Florence', 'The Last Scene of the Death of Marguerite de Bourgogne', or 'A Secret of Philip the Prudent, King of Spain'. Or metaphysical: one of Flaubert's favourite characters is the Devil, who shows the world and its glories only to demonstrate that, on closer acquaintance, it is really hell.

These historical sketches are interspersed with more contemporary vignettes, such as 'A Portrait of Lord Byron', aphorisms like those of his beloved French *moralistes* (especially La Bruyère), and the observation of 'types'. One example is 'The Woman of the World', a series of numbered paragraphs in which the said woman enumerates her diabolical triumphs ('In bygone days, in the time of the Caligulas and the Neros, I howled in the arena, I came to aid Messalina in her obscene tortures, I cut down the Christians, and I roared in the Coliseum with the tigers and the lions'). The author wrote this on the night of 1st–2nd June 1836, 'in less than half an hour' – which shows how fluently Flaubert's imagination recurred to a bloody and brutal antiquity. He was devoted to the more picturesque Roman emperors; he loved Suetonius's *Lives of the Caesars*; he wrote of his 'profound veneration for the tyrannical regimes of ancient times', and viewed them as 'mankind's finest achievement'. Nero was 'the culminating point of the ancient world'.

'Bibliomania' is a short tale (based on a true story) that depicts a Catalonian book dealer who murders the very clients who have bought his rare books, which he cannot bear to part with. The main interest in the story lies in the detail that Giacomo, the bookseller, is illiterate. He dotes on his books for their physical beauty, even though their script is just a series of enigmatic traces; – and Gustave is already exploring the tension between language as transparent opening onto the world, and as opaque object within it. Giacomo is surrounded by a wealth (of information, of meaning) with which he can do nothing, and which he can merely collect and contemplate, fetishistically.

In 'Quidquid volueris', the main character, Djalioh, is half-man, half-ape, the product of an enforced mating between a black woman and an orang-utan – an experiment carried out by a French aristocrat, Paul de Monville, living in Brazil. De Monville returns to France with his creature, who is turned into a freak show. At de Monville's wedding, Djalioh, who is incapable of expressing himself in speech, grabs a violin and, smiling stupidly, scrapes out shrill melodies, arpeggios, and octaves that 'ascend like a Gothic spire'. At this party, de Monville, in response to his friends' prurient curiosity about Djalioh's sexuality, tells them: 'I once took him to a brothel, and he fled, taking with him a rose and a mirror.' Djalioh finds that only in murder can he fully express himself.

On the whole, the young Gustave's imagination preferred to dwell, not in the here and now, but in the past and in outer (or psychological) space; but there are exceptions. One of the most interesting of these is the short piece 'A Lesson in Natural History. The genus *Commis*'. (A *commis* is a clerk, shop assistant, or salesman.) It was published in *Le colibri* (*The Humming Bird*) on 30th March 1837. 'From Aristotle to Cuvier, from Pliny to M. de Blainville, huge strides have been made in the science of nature. [...] But no man has hitherto dreamt of speaking of the *Commis*, the most interesting animal of our time.' How could this animal be classified? Was it a three-toed sloth? A howler monkey? A jackal? Fortunately, our intrepid author has ventured into several offices (at his own expense – subscriptions, please!) to observe this fascinating beast, aged between thirty-six and sixty, small and chubby, with silver glasses and handkerchief. It enjoys a cheap cigar, dreams of being a soldier, never goes out without an umbrella, and is a fervent supporter of the July Monarchy. It spends its days copying documents, bent over its desk, writing slowly and savouring the smell of the ink as it darkens the pages. A portrait of the author... No, but an anticipation of *Bouvard and Pécuchet*, and a derisory caricature of how the freest, most imaginative of lives (that of the literary artist) could coincide with that of the most platitudinous of bourgeois. (In 1866, Flaubert told the Goncourts that there were two men in him; the one was a narrow-chested scribbler forever bent over a table; the other was a cheerful *commis de voyage*, or travelling salesman. It is as if the only choice in life were between being a *commis*, and being a *commis*.)

A notebook he kept between 1838 and 1841 contains 'thoughts' such as these: 'An incomprehensible thing: the infinite – but who doubts it?' – crossed out with the dismissive comment '*bête*', or 'stupid'. 'I would like to be at the gates of Paris with five hundred thousand barbarians and burn down the whole city, what flames what ruin, what ruin of ruins – .' The link between the frustrations of *bêtise* (one's own, that of others) and vengeful dreams of violence could hardly be clearer: when his vision came true in 1870–1, as the Prussians bombarded Paris and the Communards burnt it, he was aghast; but also said he would rather the city go up in flames than surrender.

Could love save our hero from his destructive broodings? A work Flaubert wrote in 1842, *November*, dwelt on the temptations of sexual love, but its autumnal title (and tone) suggests that these have already been consigned to the past. Pastness is one of its themes, as the protagonist realises that his most authentic feelings are not on the same sublime height as those of his literary paragons, they are simply duplicates of them. 'I had thought myself their equal and was now merely their copyist!' Although he never published *November*, and called it 'a sentimental and amorous ratatouille', he later read it aloud to selected friends. He read it, as a gift-offering after a row, to his lover Louise Colet, hoping that it would help her understand his *ennui*. She compared it to Chateaubriand's *René* – a flattering comparison, but Flaubert, who perhaps did not like to be reminded of the secondariness that the work explored with such incisiveness, flared up at this 'profanation' (of *November*? Or of *René*?). He re-read it in 1853 and told Louise it was full of 'monstrosities of bad taste' and he was relieved he had never sent it to the printer's: it could stay in the box, with the first *Sentimental Education*. When he read it to his father, Dr Flaubert was cool in his appraisal. Hungarian film director Gabriel Pascal met Visconti in 1935: the two talked of making a film based on *November*, to be produced by Alexander Korda. The plan came to nothing.

By this time, he had started to write with more care and less fluency. In the year he turned eighteen, while still at school, he wrote to Ernest Chevalier to complain that he now sometimes dried up. 'As for writing, I'm not doing any, or almost none, I'm happy just constructing outlines, creating scenes, dreaming of disconnected, imaginary situations, in which I float and then dive.' He was starting to see his literary activity from the outside; to pause a little, to take stock, to slow down. He was writing scenarios for works that he might, or might not, fill out. No longer would the act of writing follow so directly upon the desire to write.

He added (the words, in their deliciously understated way, can stand as an *envoi* to the magnificent productivity of his entire childhood and youth): 'My head's a crazy world!'

Élisa

Flaubert and his family usually spent their summer holidays by the sea, at the newly fashionable resort of Trouville. In later years, Parisian dandies with their yellow gloves would discover its charms; but for now it was a simple, rather isolated spot, with houses piled on top of one another, facing in all directions like a heap of shells and pebbles cast onto the shore by the waves. In August 1834, Flaubert wrote a letter to his school friend Ernest Chevalier, full of romantic effusions about sea mists and storms; but he also described how a pretty young woman (he knew, or later learned, that she was twenty-two years old) had attracted his attention – her blue eyes, the way she laughed as her husband read to her on the beach… But on returning to Pont-l'Évêque the next day, Flaubert learned that 'she had drowned, yes drowned, dear Ernest, in less than a quarter of an hour, the wave had swept her away'. She couldn't swim, and sank beneath the waves as her husband looked on, helplessly. Flaubert's tone of schoolboy facetiousness may conceal a deeper dismay. He loved rivers and the sea, and so many of his loves seem to have taken place by water; on the shores of the Mediterranean (Eulalie), by the Seine in Rouen or Paris (Louise Colet and *tutte quante*, mainly prostitutes), on the banks of the Nile (the Egyptian courtesan Kuchuk Hanem) and the Thames (if, as some have said, he was the lover of Juliet Herbert) – or by the Atlantic. Yet he seems to have had frequent nightmares about drowning: water as both love and death.

Two years later, in the summer of 1836, on the same stretch of the Normandy coast, Flaubert was walking along the beach one morning when he noticed a red pelisse with black stripes lying there on the sand – already the waves were teasing its silky fringes: maybe they would sweep it away. He went over and moved the soft, light garment out of reach of the foaming tide. Later, at lunch, a woman came over to his table and thanked him for rescuing her pelisse. It was like an apparition – the beautiful woman gazing at him with her warm eyes; she had an aquiline nose, and her upper lip was shaded by a fine down that added a certain masculine energy to her face. Her voice was modulated, musical and gentle; she was full-figured, and seemed to dress with the casualness of an artist; – but her dress of fine white muslin revealed the soft outlines of her arms, and on the next few days he saw her swimming, and envied the soft, peaceful waves as they lapped around her full breasts. She would emerge from the waves to feed her four-month-old daughter. She was Élisa, twenty-six years old, known as 'Madame Maurice', the companion of Maurice Schlésinger (they would marry only later, when her first husband died, in 1840), a German music publisher who founded the *Gazette et revue musicale* (Berlioz would be a contributor). Maurice had once, while visiting Vienna at his father's behest, earned the gratitude of Beethoven (and the right to publish piano sonatas 30–32) by procuring for him a decent veal chop.

The young Flaubert's calf love for Élisa haunted his life. Later, in 1846 (the Schlésingers had by this time settled in Baden Baden), he told Louise Colet (who was naturally jealous) that it was his 'one real passion', that it had lasted from the age of fifteen to eighteen. As a student in Paris, he continued to visit the Schlésingers, and the letters he continued to write to Élisa are filled with a respectful, muted, but poignant fervour.

Memoirs of a Madman, and the second *Sentimental Education*, invest the encounter at Trouville with increasing fictional force. 'Maria' in the first story is a parallel to Élisa, so much so that

I have ignored the facts of geometry and taken some details from the *Memoirs* to adorn the account above of the meeting with Élisa. The archetypal resonances (Venus Anadyomene, fantasies of drowning – the dark harbinger who had been swept away a couple of years earlier – and rebirth from the waters, together with tales of imperilled damsels and gallant rescuers) override whatever facts there are. The elevation of Élisa into an inaccessible ideal love, which made all others insipid (Flaubert remarked, at an age when he had considerable sexual experience, that all his mistresses were merely mattresses: he was still, in the real sense of the word, a virgin), suggests that his vision of her arrested him, froze him into a posture of helpless, distant, feudal devotion. The 'madness' of this love is indicated in the title of the first shrine he built to her. But it was Élisa who really went mad: years later, in the summer of 1863, he learned from Maxime Du Camp that she had been 'locked away in an asylum'. He had seen her, in Baden Baden, looking thin, white-haired, wild-eyed, out for a walk, leaning on the arm of her son. In October 1872, Flaubert wrote to her: 'My old Friend, my old Love, I cannot see your handwriting without being moved.' And then, curiously (his mother had died in April that year): 'I would so much like to receive you *in my home*, to make you sleep in my mother's bedroom.' But their relationship was essentially, right from the start, one of memory. As she was something past, he could love her without any hope (perhaps without any desire) of being loved in return. 'I'm an *Old Man*. The future has no more dreams for me. But bygone days appear as if bathed in a golden haze. – Against that glowing background on which beloved ghosts hold out their arms to me, the face which stands out most splendidly is yours! – Yes, yours. Ah, poor Trouville.' He once told the Goncourts that, at one of his meetings with Élisa, she had just been about to yield to him when he felt a sudden need to go to the toilet. She died in the asylum.

Alfred Le Poittevin

Alfred was a friend of the Flauberts, five years older than Gustave. He was fragile (afflicted by tuberculosis and gonorrhoea), sensitive, decadent, with bent shoulders and a somewhat haunted expression. He had an interest in philosophy (he read Kant and Spinoza closely) and fornication. He acted as a profane *psychopompos*, leading Gustave into the brothels of Rouen; he and Gustave indulged – as was common in Flaubert's circle of masculine acquaintances – in gay joshing, signing off letters with 'Farewell, my dear pederast', 'I kiss your Priapus', 'I embrace you and socratise you'. He and Gustave created for themselves an 'ideal hothouse' in which the 'dullness of life' was heated up to a temperature of 70 degrees Reaumur (= 200 degrees Fahrenheit, as Homais would have put it); Alfred's long metaphysical poem *Bélial* dealt with evolutionism and reincarnation, and he wrote poems on themes close to Flaubert's heart, notably one on Saint Simeon Stylites. (Osip Mandelstam would refer to Flaubert, not altogether approvingly, as a Saint Simeon of style.) But even this most romantic and 'transcendental' of Flaubert's friends was soon starting to hover precariously close to earth. Flaubert urged him not to marry, not to have children, to reduce his affections to the smallest circumference – 'lay yourself open as little as possible to the enemy'. (This was in a letter in which Flaubert detailed the death of his beloved sister.)

Alfred died twice, as far as Flaubert was concerned: once when he married, and once when he died. Gustave watched as Alfred gradually floated down from the ivory tower towards the mire at its feet. 'Are you sure, great man, that you won't end up becoming bourgeois? I associated you with all my artistic hopes.' In his mid-twenties, he told Colet: 'the greatest events of my life have been a few thoughts, reading, certain sunsets by the sea at Trouville, and conversations of five or six hours in succession with a friend [Alfred] who is now married and lost to me.' But Alfred did not live long to enjoy the amenities of life, bourgeois or otherwise. When Flaubert realised that Alfred was dying, he wrote to Louise that if he ever wrote his memoirs, Alfred would occupy a large place in them. Together with Du Camp, Gustave visited Le Poittevin at his home; Alfred, although wan and struggling to breathe, rallied enough to join them on a country walk on which they discussed politics; but the force with which a man persists in existing is limited, and infinitely surpassed by the power of external causes; and – having spent his last days reading Spinoza – Alfred passed away on 3rd April 1848.

Flaubert sat up keeping vigil over Alfred's corpse for two nights; on the first night, he read Creuzer's *The Religions of Antiquity* (one of the main sources for *The Temptation of Saint Anthony*), and, on the second, Hugo's *Autumn Leaves*. The putrefaction of Alfred's body (his running fluids soiled the sheets) was a fact on the same level as the upsurge of 'joy and freedom' that Flaubert felt on his friend's behalf when the corpse was wrapped in two shrouds, making him look like 'an Egyptian mummy'.

After Alfred's death, Flaubert was 'horror-stricken' to read Balzac's novel *Louis Lambert*, the story of a man 'who goes mad by thinking of intangible things'; Gustave recognised Alfred, and many of the things they had said and done together, in the novel. Mummified, released into death, Alfred continued to accompany Flaubert; he was with Gustave, bizarrely, at his (Alfred's) funeral; he was in the song of the birds. Alfred's sister Laure was the mother of Guy de Maupassant, who was to be

Flaubert's disciple (and the creator of many ghost stories of his own). In 1862, Gustave wrote to her that, although he knew 'what are commonly called "the most intelligent men of the period"', he found them mediocre in comparison with Alfred; he remembered their voyages together into the wild blue yonder of metaphysics, admitted the depth of his jealousy when Alfred married, and said that he still thought of him constantly.

A few years before, Le Poittevin had made a brilliant start as a lawyer; it was into this profession that Flaubert, with considerable misgivings, initially followed him.

Law

In 1841, Flaubert registered as a law student in Paris. He had already imagined it all, at the age of seventeen, when Ernest Chevalier had left Rouen and gone to the capital to study law. It must be a 'lovely, carefree existence', he told Ernest: glasses of kirsch, plenty of nicotine and alcohol, masked balls, champagne, liqueurs and prostitutes – a whole wild orgy (no need for details, 'I'll take that as read'): 'Howling! Bellowing! Roaring!' But would Flaubert, the 'sullen dreamer', the 'aimless creature' that he was, bother to relive those clichés? He had already been to the brothel ('boring' – not his usual response), tobacco gave him a sore throat (but he continued to smoke heavily), and he'd soused himself quite often enough.

He took rooms in the Latin Quarter; first at 35, rue de l'Odéon, then at 19, rue de l'Est, overlooking the Luxembourg Gardens. His allowance was not enough for him to live in style: he ate in a greasy spoon on the rue de La Harpe. And he was soon feeling oppressed by his studies. Physically, as he said himself, he would have made an excellent lawyer: he had a strong pair of lungs, and stood six feet tall; he rather relished the idea of defending some notorious criminal in court. But he was unable to *get into law*. He soon found that, instead of studying his subject, he was studying his fellow-students, with an increasing wonderment at their ambitions, their raw enthusiasms, and their obtuseness. He hated legal jargon's lack of style – and it is at this point that the word 'style' starts to make a more frequent appearance in his letters, as if real style would henceforth reside in whatever lay outside the law. 'A lovely subject, Law! Dammit, what fine styles they have, MM. Oudot and Ducoudray! […] To think that for a whole month I haven't read a line of poetry, listened to a note of music, peacefully dreamt for three hours at a stretch, or lived for a single minute!' The Law was even invading his dreams – and 'I was ashamed at the dishonour thus done to dreaming'.

He had made a start on the *Code civil* but claimed he could not understand its title page. He read the first three articles of the *Institutes* and then immediately forgot what they contained. He fled to Trouville, swam in the sea, read Rabelais (who had parodied legal language – and pretty much every other kind of technical jargon – in *Gargantua* and *Pantagruel*): but then had to return, feeling as pickled as a gherkin in vinegar. He socialised, and even met Victor Hugo, one of the idols of his childhood, but this paradoxically provided no escape from things juris-prudential: the two men talked together animatedly (and indeed dominated the conversation), but for some strange reason their talk was all of 'punishment, revenge, thieves'.

Gustave's method of study consisted of blindly copying out page after page from the legal textbooks. Despite the availabil-ity of prostitutes, he lived chastely. He told Ernest Chevalier (in words that might provoke a flicker of interest in the eyes of a Lacanian analyst) that studying law left him in a state of 'moral castration'; and, standing outside a shop in the rue Vivienne, he was tempted to act out this fantasy and take a knife to his manhood. Soon he was 'in a state of prodigious annoyance [*embêtement*]'; he had reached section XIV of Book II of the *Institutes* and still had the whole *Code Civil* to work through. 'God all-fucking-shitting-mighty' (and similar expostulations), 'may the Devil strangle jurisprudence and those who invented it!' He detested the quiddities, quillities, cases, tenures and tricks of the law: how could anyone create Literature from *that*? Anyone using the words *usucapion, agnats, cognats* ('give me cognac any day!') should themselves be hauled up before the courts. At a dinner with the Portuguese ambassador, he was suddenly seized by the temptation (apparently unmotivated) to give the man a good thrashing. He roared and stamped and yawned. He writhed around amid his piles of notes, as if he had St Vitus's dance, or the falling sickness. And then he fell.

The sickness

After the meeting with Élisa, his sudden attack of sickness was the second event which set its stamp on Flaubert's development. It happened during the winter vacation (not long previously, he had failed his law exams, and would need to re-sit them). He was back in Normandy, and on New Year's Day, 1844, he and his brother Achille were returning at night from Deauville, where their father was planning to build a new cottage on family property. Flaubert was driving the two-wheeled cabriolet down the dark country road; a waggoner was coming up on the right, and suddenly he was swept off in an explosion of light, a 'torrent of flames'. He fell to the floor of the cabriolet; Achille hurriedly took him to a nearby farmhouse and bled him. Gustave was then driven home, where his father took over the treatment; only after Gustave had been bled three times did he finally open his eyes. While trying to raise a vein for the bleeding, his father accidentally scalded Flaubert's right hand, leaving it with a lifelong scar.

A few weeks later, Flaubert wrote a letter to Ernest Chevalier in which he described his attack as 'a brain congestion, i.e. a kind of miniature apoplectic fit accompanied by nervous disorders which I'm going to hang on to because it shows good taste'. It had been a brush with death: he had almost gone off to see 'Pluto, Rhadamanthys and Minos'. And he was still in an awful state: 'at the least sensation all my nerves quiver like the strings on a violin, my knees, my shoulders and my belly tremble like leaf. Anyway, such is life, *sic est vita, c'est la vie.*' His neck was swathed in stiff *seton* dressing, and he was having to swallow great quantities of pills and tisanes, and follow a diet – 'a thousand times worse than all the illnesses in the world'. He even had to give up his pipe, temporarily.

The attack, and those that followed, irregularly, through the years, has no clear diagnosis. Maxime Du Camp, in the memoirs he published after Flaubert's death, caused considerable resentment among Flaubert's friends and family by calling it what it most obviously resembles: epilepsy – for the falling sickness was still a *mal sacré*, the object of superstitious fear and revulsion. The weight of current medical opinion concurs with Du Camp. The phosphenes that inaugurate seizures were described with characteristic precision by Flaubert: 'Within a single second a million thoughts, images, combinations of every kind burst in my brain all at once like all the rockets of a firework display', and he also evoked the cascade of ideas, the ecmnesic hallucinations, and the aphasia that preceded the fall into unconsciousness. Further indications include long periods of hypoactivity interrupted by paroxysms of impulsiveness and anger: Flaubert, in short, seems to have suffered from a complex partial epilepsy, occipital-temporal in origin.

There have been dissenting voices. Sartre claimed that the illness was psychogenic, the somatisation of a neurosis (and thus a form of hysteria – after all, didn't Flaubert, in a letter of 12th January 1867, call himself an old hysteric?). Flaubert was responsible for it; he *chose* to be ill.

There is some evidence that, willed or not, the illness came to Flaubert as a release, and that, in some obscure sense, there was an element of make-believe in it. From childhood, Flaubert had been an accomplished mimic. Rather than having ideas of his own, he loved to place ideas into the mouths (or minds) of his fictional characters and then report them, sometimes directly, sometimes in the form known as free indirect speech. He played with the idea of being an actor: the novelist's trade was another way of speaking the words of others, of *being* others, irresponsibly. That way (as he wrote during the writing of *Madame Bovary*) he could stop being himself and 'circulate' (an image he loved) through the whole of his creation – he could be Emma and Rodolphe in the forest, and their horses, the autumn leaves, the wind in the trees, the words they spoke to each other. There were dangers in this process: the lovemaking between Emma and Rodolphe had made him sweat and his throat tighten; he was in a state of 'complete Illusion', and 'just as I was writing the words *attack of nerves*, I was so carried away, I was yelling so loud, and I was feeling so deeply the sensations of my little woman [Emma], that I was afraid I might have an attack myself.' (The phrase 'attack of nerves' survived into the final version of *Madame Bovary*, but not to describe Emma's erotic bliss with Rodolphe – rather, her later explosion of fury against Charles.) Flaubert's other illnesses also had a mimetic moment in them. In April 1876, he wrote that he had been suffering from a *'zona'* or attack of shingles – *'mal des ardents*, Saint Anthony's fire' – an apt disease, since that troubled saint, the patron of those suffering from ergotism (and epilepsy), was still preoccupying him.

He also told Louise Colet that, while a teenager, he had enjoyed mimicking a particular person he met on the beach at Trouville – a down-and-out ex-journalist and epileptic, who told Gustave his story. Flaubert's father had told him to stop, but Gustave remembered the occasion with zest: 'There's no doubt about it; while I was mimicking that fellow, I really got into his skin' – and really looked hideous! He was mocking the afflicted; the wind changed.

Flaubert also referred to his 'charlatanesque' character; his imitations of others could be amusing or tiresome. He devoted considerable effort, on the Nile, to imitating the cry of the camel, with its idiosyncratic mixture of gurgle and yowl: Du Camp found this aspect of him 'puerile'. But in his years at court, Gustave also observed closely the gait of Emperor Napoleon III (whom he once dismissed as an example of 'pure stupidity'), and, wearing his dressing gown, he took him off, with great effect, for the benefit of Zola: 'a classic emperor,' noted Edmond de Goncourt, 'with his dragging step [*au pas traînant*], one hand behind his bent back, twisting his moustache, uttering idiotic phrases of his own invention'. This was in 1875; Zola's novel of the Franco-Prussian War, *The Debacle*, published in 1892, contains some striking vignettes of the stricken, defeated Napoleon III; perhaps they are partly indebted to Flaubert's performance.

Flaubert was grateful for his illness. It relieved him of the need to continue staring in dull hebetude at the implacable paragraphs of the *Code civil*. Eventually he could live as a *rentier*, off the income from the substantial property he would inherit from his father. However, he would always be subliminally aware that another attack could happen at any time, perhaps when he was far from home (as happened in Egypt, for example); later moments of absent-mindedness might segue into real *absences*, as perhaps occurred when, in mid-life, he was nearly run over by a train. (This did not stop the Goncourts, who saw themselves as sickly, nervous, over-sensitive urbanites, from waxing indignant at the rude good health this country boy seemed to enjoy, with his ruddy cheeks and his booming voice: he seemed positively vulgar.)

Flaubert decided, in fact, that his attack could count as a rebirth: it cut his life into two, before, and after, the attack. 'He who is now living – as me – merely contemplates the other one, who is dead.' He viewed the ordinary world with a new intensity, as if it might explode into stars at any minute. He was a seer who saw real and surreal as one.

Many years later, in a revelatory letter to his new penfriend Mlle Leroyer de Chantepie, he mused on how he (like she) had deliberately refused happiness and love. 'I too loved a great deal, in silence, – and then, at twenty-one, I nearly died of a nervous illness, brought on by a series of irritations and troubles, by late nights and outbursts of anger. This illness lasted for ten years.'

The late nights and anger lasted the rest of his life ('I go from exasperation to a state of collapse, then I recover and go from prostration to Fury, so that my average state is one of being annoyed').

Élisa had been an absolute love that made all later loves seem contingent (as if he need never love again); his fall had, in some deep sense, relieved him of the need to act at all. Having rejected the Law (or been rejected by it) he would serve a different law: he would be judge, he would be jury; with what relish (and what fury) he would roast human beings like chestnuts in his books! And yet the judgment passed at the end of the case of *Gustave Flaubert vs the human race* would only ever be a suspended sentence.

But perhaps he didn't need 'the fall' at all; perhaps it was simply an objective event that enabled him to endorse a decision he had made before. Even the eventhood of his illness remains dubious: just as the appearance of Élisa precipitated emotions that were already lying in wait, his fall, and the escape it offered him, was already scripted. And it is best not to be quite so blunt as Du Camp. Nobody really understands the nerves. Given Flaubert's lifelong (and stupid) obsession with stupidity, we might as well diagnose him as suffering, not from a complex partial occipital-temporal epilepsy, but from a marvellous *aberratio mentalis partialis*, type two, beautifully developed. Or from *bovarysme*. Or from that most singular of diseases, a *private language*: 'I have the infirmity that I was born with a special language to which I alone hold the key.' Or from *style*, which – he said – in the daytime made him ill, and at night-time gave him fever.

Croisset

Flaubert's father decided that a move was long overdue. His son should be taken away from the at times disturbing environment of the Hôtel-Dieu. Dr Flaubert had found the perfect place: three storeys high, in Croisset, on the outskirts of Rouen, next to the towpath of the river Seine; it was clean, spacious and quiet. It had previously been used as living quarters for a Benedictine abbey: Flaubert was moving from a building that had been devoted mainly to the cure of bodies (though the Hôtel-Dieu had also been a prison, a warehouse, and a barracks) to one that had sheltered doctors of the soul. The whole family moved in June 1844. It was to his residence in Croisset that Flaubert later invited selected friends (and from which he resolutely kept away so many others). The writers among them have left eloquent reports, which is useful, since the house itself, apart from the pretty little pavilion where the family would often assemble after dinner, was demolished shortly after Flaubert's death to make way for a distillery. The Goncourts described it as 'a pretty dwelling with a Louis XVI façade at the bottom of a slope on the riverbank of the Seine'. They also brought their overripe sensibilities to bear, a little sniffily, on Flaubert's lack of decorative sense. His art collection was a bizarre collection of bric-à-brac, they thought, with dingy watercolours and muddy oils; the master of style had even cut out pictures from magazines and boxes – and stuck them on his walls! By the time they first got to know him, his rooms also contained mementoes of his travels in the East (two mummy's feet from the grottoes in Samoun, various amulets, arrow heads and oriental musical instruments), and there was an oriental feel to most of the furnishings (the Turkish cover on the bed, the Turkish divan…) and to the way Flaubert habitually dressed while at home (capacious trousers tied round with a silk cord, an immense bathrobe or, in summer, a floating white *burnous*).

There was also a bronze bust of Hippocrates – a reminder, no doubt, of his father.

Maupassant wrote of how the five-windowed study that Flaubert occupied during his mature years looked out over the river; the boats sailed by, so close they seemed about to touch the house's walls with their yards as they silently passed downstream towards all the faraway countries you dream of. If Flaubert leaned out of the window, he could contemplate the spires and towers of Rouen to his left, while a little more to the right the factory chimneys of Saint-Sever spewed out their coils of smoke. The La Foudre fire pump rose up as high as the pyramids of Egypt, and gazed across the river at the spire of Rouen cathedral. When friends came to see him, Flaubert would take them down into the garden, and they would walk along the beautiful avenue of lime trees. Flaubert liked to think that Pascal, who had relatives in Rouen, had walked up and down here, having his thoughts. For Flaubert, Croisset was a home, a refuge, a workplace, and a system of habits to which he clung with persistence. Immanuel Kant was so regular in his daily walks that the housewives of Königsberg could set their clocks by him; as Flaubert devoted himself to his no less austere nocturnal labours, the mariners of the Seine would use the lamplight shining from his two riverside windows as a beacon. He loved to sail on the river; he also swam in it until late in life, his red face puffed out with exertion, his walrus moustache dripping.

Flaubert himself remembered the house at Croisset while sailing down the Nile in February 1850. He remembered the ice floes that would bump into the riverbank, and thought of the red, yellow, green, pink and violet buds that would just be appearing on the trees now that winter was passing into spring. He also fondly recalled the fishermen who would come to fish for calyuots in the early hours of a moonlit night in July. (*Calyuot* is a Norman word for the male of the *feinte*, a member of the Clupeides family. Norman words appear in *Madame Bovary*, perhaps a little less than might realistically be expected: one example is Binet's *'crassineux'*, referring to the 'foul' weather.) An edited version of Flaubert's Nileside musings was engraved on marble and set on the pavilion at Croisset.

His routine, after the trip to Egypt, was settled. He awoke at about 10 a.m.; a servant would bring him his ready-filled pipe, his mail, and the newspapers that Gustave frequently claimed to disdain. His mother came from her adjoining bedroom to chat, before a late breakfast with niece Caroline and her nurse. On fine days, they would go for a walk. In the afternoon, after giving Caroline a little private tuition, he would start work. Dinner was at seven. He worked late into the night.

Maxime Du Camp

Flaubert had already met Maxime Du Camp before his illness and the move to Croisset, in March 1843. Gustave sealed his friendship with this tall, slender, alert young man almost immediately, paying him the homage of reading to him his manuscript of *November*, in an overnight session which led to Du Camp enthusing about the literary talents of his new acquaintance. The two men came from similar backgrounds: Du Camp too was the son of a celebrated surgeon, and when his father died young, Du Camp inherited considerable wealth. At the age of thirteen, Du Camp attended the premiere of Vigny's *Chatterton*, that celebration of childhood genius (and fakery); he was so overcome by what he was seeing on stage that he fainted. On coming round, he burst into tears. He attended the prestigious lycée Louis-le-Grand, from which he was expelled (as was Baudelaire, at about the same time – expulsion was so *chic*), and rapidly established himself as an habitué of the Paris salons. He used his inheritance to travel widely; shortly after making the acquaintance of Flaubert, he set off for the East in 1844–5. He also became Flaubert's travelling companion in Brittany and, most notably, in Egypt and Palestine in 1849–51.

Du Camp was more overtly ambitious than Flaubert; he was also ambitious for Flaubert. Both of these facts caused Gustave some irritation. It was not merely his mother who was constantly urging him, even after the onset of his illness, to get a proper job, but Du Camp too, forever encouraging him to move to Paris in the Balzac-accredited, talented-young-man-from-the-provinces-making-his-mark-on-the-capital way. Flaubert demurred, grouchily and at times defensively. Du Camp also tried to jolt Flaubert out of his fixation on the past. Why dwell among sarcophagi and old heresies when there was a whole modern world out there to capture in fiction? Alfred Le Poittevin was a bad influence, Du Camp decided: a decadent and a dreamer. (Alfred seems in retrospect something of a precursor of Husymans' hero Des Esseintes: he even called himself a 'Greek of the Late Empire' – and boasted that he would give all of Horace's odes in exchange for one chapter of Apuleius.)

Du Camp would be largely responsible for forcing the reluctant Flaubert into the public eye. Maxime saw *Madame Bovary* into print; in 1851, he refounded the *Revue de Paris*, and it was in the pages of that important, experimental and at times subversive journal that the story of Emma Bovary would first be published. (Baudelaire thought that Du Camp was the only 'man of action' on the *Revue de Paris*, 'more intelligent than the whole gang', and the only one who had ever been of use to him personally. He dedicated the last poem in *Les Fleurs du Mal* to him.)

Du Camp (whom Flaubert admired for his 'heroism' and his 'delicacy') was much more of the man of action and initiative than Flaubert: Buck Mulligan to Stephen Dedalus, perhaps. He and Flaubert were both present at the events of 1848, but Du Camp was far the more adventurous, joining the *Garde Mobile* (dominated, according to Karl Marx, not by wealthy bourgeois like Du Camp but by the *Lumpenproletariat*), laying siege to a barricade in the Faubourg Possonnière, and getting himself shot in the leg. In 1853 he was awarded the *Croix d'honneur*. By this time, he and Flaubert had quarrelled. Gustave wrote to him that they were no longer travelling in the same direction; he, Flaubert, was not seeking port, but heading out to sea – and 'if I get shipwrecked, don't mourn me'.

Whereas Flaubert was very wary of publishing accounts of his travels, Du Camp made travel writing one of his fortes. His two-volume *Souvenirs littéraires* is the source of much information (imaginatively embroidered) on Flaubert. But just as much light is shed on the world in which Flaubert lived by Du Camp's enormous sociological study, *Paris: its organs, its functions, its life in the second half of the 19th century*, published in 1869–75, and thus in the period just following Flaubert's *Sentimental Education* of 1869. (Walter Benjamin's unfinished *Passagenwerk*, on Paris as the 'capital of the nineteenth century', quotes Du Camp frequently – much more than it does Flaubert.) In his work, Du Camp traces *la vie parisienne* from the cradle to the grave, via the brothel, the police station, the penitentiary, the poor house, the hospital, and the morgue. In the section devoted to 'La Guillotine', he accompanies the group sent to take the condemned prisoner to the scaffold. He informs us that every girl sent to the notorious prison of Saint-Lazare, however innocent, emerges corrupted and vice-ridden. On one of his data-collecting visits here, he is given two mass-books belonging to a girl just sixteen years old. She has been here for six months, at her father's request. As he leafs through the pages, Du Camp notes that she has written her own thoughts between the liturgical lines, sometimes including dates, so that the process of her degradation – as she succumbs to the torrid and 'unnatural' desires of a Sappho – can be tracked. He notes, laconically, 'Saint Anthony in his desert was not tortured more intensely.'

Du Camp also trains his investigative gaze on the treatment of madness in nineteenth-century France. Theatres and novels, he claims, convey a false, over-romanticised view of this phenomenon: instead of madness being a state of delirium and unbridled fantasising, the mad person is generally a 'monomaniac' who is perfectly sane on every topic except for one overriding *idée fixe*. Du Camp was shown a four-volume quarto manuscript: it was a compendium, together with commentary, of everything written on the subject of madness by Greek, Latin, German, English,

Italian and French authors. It was a methodical and lucid work. It had been compiled by a madman – or at least, by a former inhabitant of the asylum at Charenton, an ex-magistrate who sometimes froze, mute, terrified, as cavalry squadrons charged full tilt towards him.

The inhabitants of one of the asylums seem hardly human. With their low brows and lifeless eyes, their 'drooping, slavering lips, their random gesticulations, their staggering gait', they resemble 'young bears standing on their rear paws'. They are objects of amazement and compassion. From some of the isolation cells, he hears the constant clamour of howling, yapping, roaring. Many of the inmates are aphasic, but some can utter a few words, and there is even a primary ('very primary') school at the asylum in Bicêtre, for 'young idiots'. Their devoted teacher, M. Deleporte, tries to bring some light into these dark minds – a truly Sisyphean task, since almost all his pupils are epileptics. At the first attack of the *mal sacré* they forget everything they have just learned. As their convulsions begin, they are taken away to a large, airy room, well-padded with mattresses: but some still suffer such violent falls that their heads have to be encased in rubber. At carnival time, the director of one of the asylums, at La Salpêtrière, arranges for a magician to come and put on a little show for the girls and women who are mad or epileptic: they gaze in silence at the 'théâtre ambulant' he has set up. Du Camp even attended a masked ball at which the madwomen were dressed up as marquises, milkmaids and Pierrots. On the whole, he did not demur from the judgement that epileptics were frequently best looked after in such institutions. (In the Salpêtrière, as Charcot discovered, epileptics were confined in the company of the retarded and the criminally insane, as well as those with chronic syphilis.)

As well as scrutinising the population of Paris, Du Camp also detailed its railway stations and its markets. He dragged Flaubert out one chilly night in March 1868 to survey Les Halles. After a few hours' observation in the company of his ever-inquisitive friend, Flaubert, frozen stiff, went off to bed at 3 a.m. Du Camp's account of Les Halles in *Paris* would prove useful to later novelists such as Zola (who however also supplemented it with considerable fieldwork of his own). And then there were the aqueducts that provided the thirsty capital with its fresh water. During the Franco-Prussian war, there were fears that the enemy might sabotage these aqueducts, and indeed they did divert the water of one (though the structure itself was not damaged). This was the great Dhuis aqueduct (it now serves Eurodisney). Du Camp was filled with admiration at the sight of the reservoir that fed the aqueduct: it is 'one of the most impressive spectacles' imaginable. Indeed, although he had seen the cistern of Ezechias in Jerusalem, and the well of Solomon at Raiz-el-Aïn (between Bethlehem and Maar-Saba), the Dhuis reservoir far surpassed them: its engineer, Belgrand, can be sure of his reputation, and say with the poet Horace *I shall not wholly die*.

All this lay in the future. For the time being, as young men, Flaubert and Du Camp were content to dream. They would wait until they were forty and retire to the countryside together; they would burn the midnight oil, they would acquire enormous erudition; – and their days would follow one another in tranquil and studious succession, after which they would make their names with a vast philological work on modern languages, called *The Transmigrations of Latin*.

Flaubert and Du Camp set off on a walking tour of the Loire, Brittany and Normandy. They carried knapsacks on their backs, slept rough, sometimes dined on eggs and bread. They wrote a book about it – Maxime did the even chapters, Gustave the odd. It was not published during their lifetimes; Flaubert told Louise Colet that it was 'quite exact in its descriptions', but basically 'pure fantasy', laden with digressions. It was yet another encounter with self-doubt and the threat of over-fastidious stylistic compunction. 'I hesitate, I start to worry, I feel resentful, I feel afraid, my sense of good taste increases as my verve decreases.'

On his tour, Flaubert communed with the dead. Brittany in particular, with its archaeological remains, its many little churches, graveyards and elaborate calvaries, was haunted land – a foreign country when compared to Paris and environs. Despite his sense of the otherness of the landscape, Flaubert was already turning a beady eye on cultural heritage, as well as zestfully mimicking another set of technical terms: 'dolmens! And menhirs! And peulvens! And galgals! And barrows!', he wrote to Ernest Chevalier, adding 'there's nothing more tedious than Celtic archaeology, it's all so desperately similar'. But he composed a mock treatise on the subject – and his chapters in the co-authored *Through Fields and Strands* demonstrate how his nerves picked up, with a mixture of suspicion and fascination, the uncanny vibrations of something odd, ancient, numinous. In Landerneau he saw a dog running through the streets. It was half-crazed; there was a saucepan attached to its tail.

Deaths

As his father's son, and his brother's brother, Gustave could hardly avoid being preoccupied with disease and mortality. Death was not a problem: he had died many times already, and for such a pessimist, the prospect was not unattractive. But disease and decrepitude could be more troublesome. From the time of his nervous attack onwards, he suffered from abscesses, carbuncles, inflammations and other assorted ailments. At the age of twenty-five he told Louise Colet that he considered himself to be an old man. At thirty, he thought of himself as forty, or fifty, or sixty. At the age of thirty-one he was losing his hair and his teeth. To these ills he would add, picked up probably during his travels in the East, syphilis. The treatment for this (and one of the treatments his father tried on him after his attack) involved mercury, which often killed the patient with the disease. By the time he was fifty, all his teeth except one had fallen out (turning him into a baleful masculine Norn), and his saliva was as black as his bile. But long before that, he was feeling middle-aged or even senescent. He certainly had a medieval sense of the ills which flesh is heir to: 'throughout our lives we are nothing but corruption and putrefaction'.

Sometime in late 1845, Dr Flaubert probably dropped a scalpel while dissecting a corpse. It grazed his leg, infecting it. The wound turned septic, and despite the ministrations of his son Achille, who operated in an attempt to drain the pus, he died in January 1846. He left his son a wealthy man (almost a sterling millionaire, perhaps, in today's terms).

Six weeks later, Flaubert's sister Caroline gave birth to a daughter, also named Caroline, before succumbing to puerperal fever. Flaubert had greeted the news of his sister's imminent marriage by saying 'Ah!' Now, keeping vigil over her dead body with her distraught husband Émile, he sat revolving many memories (their childhood playing together in the garden near the dissecting room; his fling with Eulalie Foucaud) and reading Montaigne. There was a priest snoring away in the corner. Flaubert thought: 'all things pass away'. And: 'the idea alone remains'. A death mask was taken of her face; later, the sculptor Pradier made a bust of her, which adorned Flaubert's study. When she was buried, it was discovered that the grave was too small for her coffin; the gravedigger had to stamp the coffin down, at the place where Caroline's head was. Flaubert was – as he wrote to Du Camp – dry-eyed, but horribly irritable. Now he had to look not only after his grieving and valetudinarian mother ('a weeping statue'), but also his niece, baby Caroline, who was a sickly child. Madame Flaubert, with the help of Gustave, rallied enough to devote herself to the infant. Flaubert later wrote: 'Before the deaths of my father and sister, I'd attended their burial, and when the event actually happened, I was already familiar with it.'

Louise Colet

The year 1846 was a year of love as well as death for Flaubert. While visiting the *atelier* of Pradier on the Quai Voltaire in Paris, Flaubert saw a beautiful young woman posing for the sculptor. She had an intelligent, somewhat feline face and the same ringlets of hair as his dead sister Caroline. Her name was Louise Colet; from Aix-en-Provence, she was already a published poet of some repute, and had married and produced a daughter. Her fierce independence of spirit, her leftwing politics, and her restless vitality would attract considerable opprobrium: the Catholic dandy writer Barbey d'Aurevilley (who would also be a waspish, spiteful, at times insightful critic of Flaubert) paid her the honour of calling her 'violent', 'outrageous', a 'Jacobin'; she was a 'bluestocking' of red politics, a revolutionary 'gargoyle', a dishevelled, bloodthirsty Sibyl, a 'turbulent, imprecatory, and frothy Muse'. Paris intellectuals said she was vain, self-publicising – and hysterical! Although married, she also maintained a complex, fraught relationship with Victor Cousin (an 'eclectic' thinker who was fatefully responsible for introducing the ideas of Hegel into France): when she became pregnant by him, the couple were lampooned in print by the journalist Alphone Karr (who later captured the sense of general disillusionment following the failure of the 1848 revolutions by coining the phrase *'plus ça change, plus c'est la même chose'*). Colet, big with child, attacked him with a kitchen knife, but drew just a few drops of blood.

The speed at which she could write was legendary: it was said that she composed her verse drama on Charlotte Corday in twenty-four hours. Her liaison with Flaubert was bound to be stormy (liaisons: always stormy), but it began with the usual mutual fascination.

He was twenty-four, she was thirty-six; he was taken by her air of experience, and was soon calling round on her to listen as she read from her translation of Shakespeare's *The Tempest* into alexandrines (he preferred the sections she had rendered in prose). They talked of her poetry, too; Flaubert, ever the professional, managed to praise a turn of phrase here and a metaphor there but complained about a general slackness, a lack of concision and verbal energy, a tendency to go for the *à peu près*. Nevertheless, they soon became lovers. Sartre and others have pondered long and hard whether this happened in a coach ride through the Bois de Boulogne, and whether Flaubert's stage fright the first time (he told Louise that *it had never happened before* – in any case, he soon made up for it) was symptomatic of some deeper Oedipal-existential angst. But Flaubert's love letters to Louise, although affectionate and even passionate, were soon backtracking. He was alienated from the world; in fact, he was already dead, and she was dragging him back, all unwilling, into life. To prove his point, after one of their encounters, he purchased a Jacques Callot engraving of the Temptation of Saint Anthony, to hang in his study. Admittedly, he sighed over her little brown slippers, and collected fetishes (such as a blood-spotted handkerchief of hers) in the time-honoured way; but he also told her that he felt old and jaded; he had his work to do; she could not come to Croisset (his ailing mother needed peace and quiet), he could not come to Paris (he needed the peace and quiet of Croisset, where he had to nurse his ailing mother and, later, his ailing novel); he would check the rail timetable and see whether he could maybe fit in a few hours to see her in Mantes, between Paris and Rouen. (His dislike of rail travel was intensified when there was a possessive mother at one end and a possessive lover at the other.)

He was soon complaining that their correspondence was 'epileptic', a word he seems to have used almost entirely metaphorically. (Years later, he would refer to Paris under siege as 'epileptic'.) She was disconcerted by his distance, aghast at the ease with which he talked of previous loves romantic or venal (Élisa, Eulalie, countless prostitutes); his attempts to reassure her backfired, for she had an active imagination. She wished for a child from him; he wrote to her in terms that suggested he was somewhat hesitant about the prospect of fatherhood: 'The hypothesis of transmitting life to anyone makes me roar, in the depths of my heart, with infernal rage.' Sometimes the post was late, and tempers flared on both sides; sometimes her period was late, and he panicked. What a relief it was when the Redcoats finally arrived, and Lord Palmerston's troops landed!

He broke off with Louise in August 1848 (Du Camp sternly rebuked her: 'From the day you first met him you have been trying to disturb his life'); but there was a reconciliation after his return from the East, just before he started *Madame Bovary*. She and Flaubert collaborated in one of the latter's rare excursions into political activism, of a kind: when Victor Hugo went into exile after the *coup d'état* of 1851, the two lovers acted as Hugo's clandestine 'letterbox' in Paris; this was not a risk-free activity, and one of Flaubert's acquaintances from schooldays in Rouen was sentenced to spend a year in jail for distributing Hugo's incendiary pamphlet on Napoléon III. In April 1854, he wrote to her revealingly: 'I've always tried (but it seems to me that I've failed) to turn you into a sublime hermaphrodite. I want you to be a man to the level of your belly (going down). You bother me and bug me and you're *spoiling yourself* with the female element.'

The relationship ended in 1855. She called round three times at his Paris apartment on 42, boulevard du Temple. He sent a last letter to her, telling her that he had not been in and '*I never will* be in'; Louise scribbled the words 'cowardly, gutless scumbag' on this dismissal. There was a world besides. She travelled, she had other loves. In Italy, in 1861, she continued to support the cause of Garibaldi and Cavour; she tried to see Pius IX, hoping to convert him to the cause of Italian unification (the Pope had proclaimed the dogma of the Immaculate Conception in 1854, and in 1864 would issue the *Syllabus of Errors* in which most of Louise's beliefs were condemned as erroneous). In St Peter's, she was repelled by the ornate tomb of Queen Christina of Sweden (in many respects her spiritual sister), and shouted into the great, echoing spaces, 'I protest against the way Christina of Sweden has been turned into a saint! [...] I much prefer Garibaldi!' She portrayed Gustave as 'Léonce', a man with 'a heart of steel' in her novels *A Soldier's Tale* and *Him, A Contemporary Novel*. Interestingly, Léonce is never seen as such, but holds aloof, sequestered on his country estate, devoted with unremitting fervour to the practice of his art. (Her novel *Him* spawned a number of similar *romans à clef*, such as George Sand's *Her and Him*, and Paul de Musset's *Him and Her*.) Louise was also a critic of colonialism, and a supporter of the Commune. In Marseille, at the age of sixty, she gave such an incendiary speech (patriotic, anti-clerical) that she provoked riots in the street. When she died, Flaubert wrote of her with distanced, melancholy affection.

As well as being productive herself, Louise acted as a Muse to many men: Flaubert wrote *Madame Bovary* with her never far from his mind. His epistolary relationship with her was crucial for his mature aesthetics.

Louis Bouilhet

If Flaubert defined himself against Du Camp, for all their friend-ship, and against his lover Louise on stylistic grounds, his rela-tionship with Louis Bouilhet was almost that of a spiritual twin. Bouilhet was a fellow pupil of Flaubert at the Collège Royal in Rouen, but it was only after the two of them had left school that they became close friends, in 1846. Bouilhet came from a much more modest family background than Flaubert; he seems to have been shy, a brilliant school student, a fine classicist, with a droll sense of humour. He aimed at first to become a doctor, and studied at the Hôtel-Dieu under Flaubert's father. He then gave up medicine in order to become a tutor; after Le Poittevin's defection to marriage and the bourgeois state, Flaubert found that Louis was a suitable replacement and confidant. Bouilhet, like Le Poittevin, had ambitions to write – and like so many in that generation, he saw literature, and the literary life, as a form of revolt. He was much closer to the *bohême* than Flaubert, who wrote to Louise Colet that Bouilhet was 'a poor lad who earns his living by giving lessons – he's a real poet, he writes superb, charming things, and he'll remain unknown because he lacks two things: bread and time.'

Bouilhet and Flaubert eventually bore a remarkably sim-ilar physical resemblance to one another: the same high fore-head, flamboyant moustache and drooping eyelids. In his letters to Louis, Flaubert adopts a very definite tone; laddish, mock-pedantic, scatological, jokily homoerotic. Flaubert was vexed, after Bouilhet's death, to discover that Louis had burnt a considerable number of the letters Gustave had sent him, 'maybe,' brooded the latter, 'because they contained a lot of filth'; and he added, 'Lewdness, which in my view is "one of the healthiest of tonics", struck him as something childish, disgusting' – and Louis had become a little prudish in his later years. But Flaubert was still grief-stricken at the passing of his comrade in letters, in 1869: Bouilhet, he told Princess Mathilde, was 'part of myself'; he called him 'my literary conscience, my judgment, my compass', and 'the one who helped me give birth, the one who could see into my thoughts more clearly than I myself'.

Flaubert was particularly impressed by Bouilhet's behaviour before his death: he died like a philosopher, reading the materialist La Mettrie, the author of *Man, a Machine*. His loyalty to his friend did not extend to putting up with the speeches given at his funeral. 'As for myself, who was at the head of the mourners, I put on a good show until the *speeches*.' In the hot sun, he fainted. Flaubert took his friend's talents seriously enough to attempt to turn his last play, 'The Weaker Sex', into a piece that could be performed; and Bouilhet's death provided the one occasion on which Flaubert's firm resolve never to commit an act of literary criticism was overridden by the pieties of friendship. He wrote a preface to Bouilhet's *Last Songs* (delicate lyrics, several on Chinese themes) in which he states that Bouilhet's 'republican faith' had been shaken by 1848 and he had become *'un littérateur absolu'*. It was the most ideological of times – not a good period for poetry to flourish in. 'In any case, style, art in itself, always appears insurrectional to governments and immoral to the bourgeois.' Bouilhet's closeness to Flaubert also comes across in the latter's comment that, out of protest against the reigning mediocrity of 'commonsense', he had taken refuge in 'vanished worlds and the Far East'. And, said Flaubert: 'He dramatised all the passions, expressed the plaints of the mummy, the triumphs of nothingness, the sadness of stones, he exhumed worlds, painted barbarous peoples, described Biblical land-scapes and wrote nursery songs': words that could, with a little editing, be applied to the man who wrote them.

The Town Council of Rouen refused to grant the space required for a fountain surmounted by a bust of Bouilhet. Flaubert had been placed in charge of raising money by sub-scription for his friend's memorial. In January 1872, he wrote a furious open letter in protest. 'With all your capital and all your wisdom, you are incapable of forming an association equivalent to the *Internationale*! Your sole intellectual effort consists in trembling at the prospect of the future. Use your imaginations! Make haste! Or else France will sink more and more between a hideous demagogy and a stupid bourgeoisie.' Bouilhet got his monument.

1848

On Christmas Day 1847, Flaubert attended a Reform Banquet in Rouen, with Du Camp and Bouilhet. His *politique des hauteurs* was offended by the copious servings of political platitudes. Hearing of the increasing unrest in Paris, he took the train there, on 23rd February 1848, to observe, 'as an artist'. The next day, they saw the pools of blood in the streets; the boulevard des Italiens was thronged by angry crowds; barricades went up, and there was fighting around the Palais-Royal. In the afternoon, a member of the *Garde Nationale* told them that Louis-Philippe had abdicated. The Tuileries were now free. Flaubert and his friends were among the first to enter; they seem to have stopped insurgents from executing a small group of soldiers in the palace gardens. The rebels shot at the mirrors. Later, the Republic was proclaimed at the Hôtel de Ville. Flaubert wondered whether it would favour Art. Indeed, he set the bar very high for the new regime: when Le Poittevin died, in April, he wrote: 'Existence is a shoddy business. I seriously doubt whether the republic will invent a remedy for it.' In May, he started work on *The Temptation of Saint Anthony*. In November, his dog died too. He wrote: 'I'm feeling more and more fed up.'

Rejection

After the encounter with Élisa and his first nervous attack, the third 'event' – which involved both Du Camp and Bouilhet – was the most wounding, and the most fateful for Flaubert's career as a writer. Its roots lay in a project that Flaubert had nursed from a very young age.

Every autumn, the Saint-Romain fair was held in Rouen: there was a carnival atmosphere (jugglers, acrobats, fire-eaters, hucksters and quacks) as the crowds milled between the tents and booths, which included little playhouses rigged up to perform playlets derived partly from the *commedia dell'arte* and partly from medieval *soties* and mystery plays. An elderly gent by the name of Albert Legrain had only one play in his repertoire, which he put on as a kind of puppet theatre: it was *The Temptation of Saint Anthony*, based very loosely on the life of Saint Anthony the Great who withdrew from world, flesh and devil to a life of contemplation in the deserts west of Thebes in Egypt. Something in Gustave responded to this abnegation, and saw the nineteenth-century artist's task as involving a similar ascesis. The Mandyn/Breughel painting catalysed these musings: he saw it in 1845, at a time when – for various reasons, possibly for fear of provoking another seizure – he avoided sexual activity, even with himself. He became obsessed by the chaste (but tempted) saint, whose temptations comprised, quite simply, the world: a pandemonium of representations that passed alluringly before him against the backdrop of the desert wastes. Among these temptations were not just the obvious ones (the Seven Deadly Sins), but also the forbidden fruits of heresy – which the young Flaubert explored with encyclopaedic zest. Not that he was tempted by heresy as such, or even by religious faith: but he had a lifelong fascination for religion. He wrote to Mlle de Chantepie: 'what draws me more than anything is religion. I mean all religions, none of them more than any other. Every dogma in particular is repellent to me, but I consider the sentiment that gave birth to them as mankind's most natural and most poetic. I really don't like philosophers who have seen nothing but imposture and stupidity in these things. Personally, I detect necessity and instinct at work there; so I respect the negro kissing his fetish just as much as the Catholic kneeling before the Sacred Heart.' So, as his vision of *Saint Anthony* expanded through the years, he would include, not just Christian heresies, but other religions, other beliefs. The 'levelling' tendency evident in the above quotation (it is not sure that either the negro or the Catholic would be pleased by a 'respect' that embraces them in a rather glib equation) is part of a general urge in Flaubert to set out all of humanity's beliefs and ideologies before him, so that he can survey them all from a position of transcendence and catalogue them as equally illusory (while feeling, like Saint Anthony, the occasional twinges of temptation – and *what if* one of them might be true, or indeed, in their different, partial ways, all of them, collectively? What if stupidity is simply taking the part for the whole?). Flaubert plunged into volume after volume of Church history and dogma, catechisms and creeds, and then inflicted them on his saint – and on his listeners. He loved reading his work aloud, and on 12th September 1849 (France was in political turmoil; the Second Republic was proving an unstable and captious entity), after three years of laborious research and writing, he asked his friends Louis Bouilhet and Maxime Du Camp to Croisset to hear him read it out, in a marathon session lasting for four days (eight hours a day). Flaubert had begged them not to deliver their verdict until it was all over. They had already huddled together, night after night: what were they going to tell him? It was the more diplomatic of the two, Bouilhet, who uttered the fateful words: 'We think you should throw it on the fire and never mention it again.'

It would be suitable, at this point, to leave a blank rather than try to imagine Flaubert's reaction (something along the lines of: a leaping to the feet, a strangled howl, a wide-eyed stare of horror, a mouth gaping open in disbelief).

In vain (or almost in vain) did they try to persuade him that he had chosen the wrong subject, that the antics of the Sphinx and the Chimaera, the wearisome procession of heretics, of Apollonius of Tyana and Montanus, of Manicheans and Marcionites and Carpocratians was a total irrelevance to modern life and that he would be better off writing something more 'down-to-earth' like a novel by Balzac. Flaubert was devastated. He later claimed that their critiques left him feeling ill for several months. As with the vision of Élisa and the New Year's gift of 1844, the event left its mark. From now on, though he would continue to subject – often to their intense pleasure – all of his friends to long readings of his work in progress (a common practice in the nineteenth century), that work would be more guarded than the first *Saint Anthony*. He would not be so naïve as to expose himself so directly again. When he did again settle down to a sustained piece of writing, it would not be the story of an isolated figure tormented by images of an unattainable fulfilment and tempted by unassuageable longings: it would be *Madame Bovary*.

Nevertheless, Saint Anthony never left him: he returned, obstinately, defiantly, to the theme, producing two more versions, of which he published only the last, in March 1874. There are touching accounts of the mixture of pride and diffidence with which he delivered to his publisher Charpentier a beautiful calligraphic version, copied out by a professional copyist from

Flaubert's manuscript, of the final *Saint Anthony*, on *de luxe* paper, swathed in ribbons of blue-grey and white, with a few extra punctuation marks added by the author in a different-coloured ink. Flaubert was paler of face than usual, his movements were slower and more deliberate, and he seemed reluctant to abandon 'his life's work' to the printers. It was published to general incomprehension – a response to which he was, by this time, relatively inured.

The East

He travelled.

Leaving Croisset and his anguished mother in the autumn of 1849 was like a death, though Flaubert claimed that the 'real' moment of emotion came when he put away his pens and papers. In Paris, he stayed with Maxime Du Camp, with whom he would be travelling to the East; Gustave spent two days recovering from the ordeal of separation by drinking and eating lavishly. He went to the opera, alone, to see Meyerbeer's *Le Prophète*. One of the greatest musical successes of the age, it is based on the Anabaptist revolt under John of Leyden in sixteenth-century Germany. But as well as dwelling, as usual, on the long history of Christian heresy, his thoughts were already turning eastwards. With Bouilhet he visited the Louvre, in particular a winged bull with a human head that had recently arrived from Nineveh, where it had been the guardian of the palace gates. There was a farewell dinner: the writer Théophile Gautier (author of tales in which the past comes uncannily alive: 'Arria Marcella', set in ancient and modern Pompeii; and 'The Mummy's Foot') was present, and encouraged Max (or, in some accounts, Flaubert) to become a Muslim so that he would be able to visit Mecca; Flaubert was more interested in discovering the sources of the Nile. Afterwards, Flaubert and Bouilhet celebrated the rites of antiquity by visiting Mère Guerin's brothel.

According to Du Camp, he and Flaubert had been given vague jobs to do by the French Government, partly to oil the bureaucratic wheels on their travels. Flaubert (to Du Camp's amusement) was supposed to collect any information that might be useful for Chambers of Commerce. Du Camp was entrusted with a mission on behalf of the Ministry of Public Instruction: he would be equipped with 'an apparatus (photographic)'. With the aid of 'this marvellous means of reproduction' ('a modern travelling companion, efficient, quick, and always scrupulously precise'), he was to take photographs of monuments and inscriptions. So Max took his camera – and Gustave (or so he later told Edmond de Goncourt) took a dozen boxes of Spanish fly with him, to offer to the local sheiks.

They had another companion too, partly because Maxime was worried about Flaubert's ill-health (and Gustave did suffer from more than one seizure during their travels): this was Sassetti, a Corsican ex-dragoon, who acted as Du Camp's manservant.

They boarded the *Nil* at Marseille. Flaubert, unlike Max, was barely sea-sick; he proved a jovial passenger, in spite of the *Saint Anthony* debacle. Some eleven days later, he was staring at a black dome rising from the horizon, set off against the blue of the Mediterranean: this was the seraglio of Abbas Pasha at Alexandria. First sights of 'the Orient': a pair of camels onshore, Arabs tranquilly fishing on the dock. First sounds: a deafening uproar, as everyone – 'negroes, negresses, camels' – kicked out at, and cudgelled, everyone and everything else. He later compared his first days in Egypt to the experience of a sleeping man suddenly finding himself hurled into the middle of a Beethoven symphony: initial hubbub followed by a gradual sense of the harmony of the whole. Although Alexandria was quite a Europeanised city, Egypt was a 'Babel' with its polyphony of languages, and the 'harsh Semitic syllables' cracking like whiplashes through the air. (He would never learn more than a few words of Arabic; what he tells us about Egypt is filtered through the rough-and-ready interpretive skills of guides and dragomans.)

And it was, above all, for this man who found that the sorrel green of Normandy could set his teeth on edge, 'a bellyful of colours'. He tried to capture the startling intensity of these colours in his notes and letters, watching, for instance, as the sunset at six in the evening made the sky look like molten vermilion and gave the desert sands an inky appearance. And not just the colours; postures, gaits, outlines – in short, *tableaux vivants* – etched themselves on his memory. Like the compilers of the great *Description of Egypt* created at the behest of Napoleon at the beginning of the nineteenth century, he carefully observed the variety of eastern costumes; where they had relied mainly on images, he described what he saw in words. Egypt sharpened his eyes: when he returned to France, he would describe its countryside, its cityscapes, the costumes and some-times the customs of the local people as if he were an explorer – from Egypt, perhaps. He was, of course, particularly struck by the differences between the dress codes of the east and those of his native land: almost all the women of Egypt were veiled, but often went bare-breasted. (At the ball at La Vaubyessard, another traveller abroad, Emma Bovary, notes that, at dinner, some of the ladies do not place their gloves in their wine glasses.)

Everyone showed respect for 'the Franks' (the French and, more generally, Europeans). The memory of 'Sultan Kebir', the 'Great Sultan', aka Napoleon, was still potent, and the 'respect' shown by the Egyptians was mingled with a certain fear. At the top of one of the pyramids in Gizeh, he later met a guide who pointed towards the sands and said, *'Napouleoun, Sultan Kebir?'*, making a chopping motion with his hands to mimic the act of beheading – perhaps an allusion to the way French troops had cut down the Mamluks who had survived the Battle of the Pyramids. On a trip to Aboukir, the travellers saw shipwrecks from the Battle of the Nile scattered on the beach; sharks had been washed up too. Flaubert and Du Camp shot 'cormorants and water-magpies'.

An Italian doctor they encountered in Rosetta gave Flaubert great pleasure – which he shared in a letter to his mother – by saying that he had heard of Flaubert's doctor father 'and even seen his name cited' in medical journals. The family name was celebrated in the Land of the Pharaohs!

They then embarked on a boat from Alexandria to Cairo. This was Flaubert's first night on the Nile: he recited some poetry by Bouilhet, and thought of Cleopatra. The next day, from the reddish-grey sands of the desert there emerged, in the distance, two pyramids and one smaller one – and then Cairo, with the dome of the mosque of Mohammed Ali.

Cairo was more foreign and exotic than Alexandria. But he still felt at home here, especially when he visited a Coptic bishop in Cairo who received him politely, and was happy to answer Flaubert's questions touching 'the Trinity, the Virgin, the Gospels, the Eucharist'. Had Flaubert come all the way to Egypt to discuss Christian theology? No: it was simply that 'all my old *Saint Anthony* erudition resurfaced'. He was in St Anthony's own country: by some miracle, this might enable him to under-stand the saint, his beliefs, and the errors he fought against more clearly. There they sat, the blue skies stretched out over their heads, books spread out all around them, the old bishop 'ruminating in his beard before replying', Flaubert sitting next to him, cross-legged, gesticulating with his pencil, taking notes; his interpreter Hassan, with his 'baggy trousers and his wide-sleeved jacket', stood immobile as he translated, and three other scholars in their black robes, sitting on stools, nodded sagely and every now and then interpreted a few words.

He was tempted by some of the 'antiques' being offered in the markets, but knew that most of them were of modern fabrication.

In Cairo, at a ceremony for the feast-day of a *santon* or Muslim holy man, he watched as a group of men assembled in a rect-angle and started to chant. A young man was caught up in the rhythm of their chanting; Flaubert noted the idiotic expression of absorption on his face. At a wedding, there was ritual clowning: a man was dressed as a woman, and jokes were exchanged about the doctor buggering his donkey out in the garden. Little girls in blue smocks made imitation farting noises with their mouths; a young boy offered to sell his mother for just five *paras*. The boy opened a jar of cakes and breathed the word 'Allah!'; Flaubert, who had found Arabic guttural, now discovered that it could sound 'charming'. He and Max moved to the Hôtel du Nil, run by two men, one of whom had once been a provincial actor: his name was Bouvaret.

There are very few photographs of Flaubert, who hated the idea of his image being propagated, and they all date from the days of his celebrity; for that very reason his face, always in the same pose, has become not just an image but an icon. It was during his stay in Egypt that his moustache became such a prominent part of his physiognomy (he also temporarily grew a beard); he was soon being called Abu-Chanab, 'Father of the Moustache', and all the whores he met told him (usually in sign language) that they disliked it, because it concealed his lovely mouth. (Most men were honorifically called 'father of something': Du Camp was 'Abu Muknaf', the 'Father of Thinness'.)

When it rained, the Arabs had to wade through the streets of Cairo, halfway up to their knees in mud, shivering with cold. Flaubert and Max visited an aqueduct on the outskirts of the city, and saw a dog tearing at the remains of a dead donkey. In the Kasr el-'Aini Hospital, they were shown several cases of syphilis, rather in the way that tourists elsewhere would visit Bedlam for an afternoon's entertainment. The doctor motioned with his hand, and the patients docilely rose to their feet and undid their belts, opening their anuses to display the chancres inside. 'One old man's prick entirely devoid of skin,' noted Flaubert; 'I recoiled from the stench.' An Arab's corpse laid out in the dissecting room had 'beautiful black hair'. He visited the local mosques with the Consul, Delaporte, who was bored by Arabic architecture but perked up considerably as they passed the negro slave market, and pointed to 'a poor negress', asking them, 'I say, do get your guide to tell her to strip.' In the Civilian Hospital of the Ezbekiyeh, there were lunatics screaming in the cells, and an old man who was begging to be beheaded. One old woman bared her drooping, skinny breasts and smiled sweetly to Flaubert as she stroked them, invitingly, while another out in the courtyard started doing handstands and showing him her arse.

Maxime took a photo of Flaubert in Bouvaret's hotel, but Gustave is distant and barely recognisable. (He was later photographed on the tip of one of the smaller pyramids at Gizeh, but this photo has been lost.) The resulting image shows the hotel garden; above it, there loom the crumbling walls with their projecting *moucharbiehs* or shuttered bay windows; against a luxuriant tangle of tall bushes, a man stands erect, in a long, flowing white cotton Nubian shirt; he seems to be sporting a thick beard and is wearing a conical hat with a white border, presumably the 'screaming red' tarboosh Flaubert referred to in his letters. His arms dangle at his side, and his head is bowed, meditatively.

In a small street behind the hotel was a brothel, where, in a large upper room, Flaubert and Max were entertained by La Triestina, who played the *darabukkah*, an elongated goblet drum with a crisp, light sound that soon intoxicates you, and makes your heart pound to its mesmerising pulse: meanwhile, another woman danced. Flaubert and this woman, Hadely, then lay down on a mat to perform a 'strange' act of coitus: Flaubert noted her shaven pubes, her firm flesh, and 'dry but fatty' cunt: the episode made him think of 'a plague victim or a leper house'. She spoke some words to him in Arabic. He did not understand, but he had always liked listening, open-mouthed, to incomprehensible languages: now they gazed into each other's eyes with redoubled intensity ('the exchange of looks is all the deeper for the curiosity and the surprise') – and anyway, 'Joseph' (Giuseppe Brichetti, a Genoese interpreter whose services they had engaged in Cairo, a rascal, in Flaubert's view, and a *bardash* or catamite as well) was there to translate, if needed. The next day (1st December 1849) Flaubert wrote to Bouilhet; after commenting gruffly that he would soon be using the ministerial instructions that lay on his desk as toilet paper, he told him that he was not much impressed by scenes of Egyptian nature, but greatly excited by the cities and the people. He appended to his letter a PS for Bouilhet's eyes alone – a little catalogue of *grotesqueries* that is justly celebrated. He tells of a jester copulating on a shop counter in the Cairo bazaar, while the shopkeeper tranquilly smokes his pipe; of a young man being calmly buggered by a monkey on the road between Cairo and Shubra; of a *marabout* (or Muslim saint) allowing himself to be masturbated dry by his women visitors; and of a *santon* who was in the habit of walking through the streets of Cairo clad in nothing but two caps, one on his head and one on his penis; when he passed water, he would remove the latter, and sterile women would come and bathe in the urine, hoping to get children. He also noted that, in Egypt, women urinated standing up, men sitting down. No he didn't: this last detail is from Herodotus – Egypt was ever, to European eyes, a land of odd habits. The status of Flaubert's list of *mirabilia* is uncertain (how many of them did he actually see, rather than hear about?), and even if they are in some sense 'authentic', the intrigued reader might want to do the anthropological homework that Flaubert neglected. He preferred to see the country as a vast collection of intense, sudden apparitions to be collected and savoured for their own sake – bizarre, alarming and captivating hieroglyphics still awaiting their Champollion. His novels show us, again and again, characters staring at scenes, or at each other, in open-mouthed incomprehension – in that most Flaubertian word of all, '*béants*': gaping, gawping. He gaped and gawped at Egypt in the same way.

At noon on Friday 7th December 1849, the party set out for the Pyramids. As their horses were being led onto the small boat that would take them across the Nile, a coffin was carried past them. The soil of the recently ploughed fields, still moist from the recent inundations, was as black as ink against the fresh green, and Flaubert was reminded of the invocation to Isis: 'Hail, hail, black soil of Egypt!' Some three hours later they were almost at the edge of the desert: the three Pyramids rose ahead of them, and Flaubert was seized by a strange frenzy, spurring his horse into a gallop and racing with Max up to the Abu-el-Houl, the Father of Terror – the Sphinx. He reined in his horse and stared at it. The Sphinx fixed them with 'a terrifying stare', and Flaubert cried aloud, 'I have seen the Sphinx fleeing toward Libya; it was galloping like a jackal. That's from *Saint Anthony.*' This moment of self-quotation was his way of making sense of the enigma ensconced in the sands, and defiantly re-asserting the validity of his art.

Du Camp, meanwhile, practised *his* art. He later boasted that he was the first person ever to photograph the Sphinx. If so, Flaubert was present at a world-historical moment: perhaps he reflected, as he looked up from his notebooks to watch as Du Camp fussed with his cumbersome apparatus and pointed its beady lens at the staring figure in the desert sands, '*that* will kill *this*'. But he later returned to the Sphinx in fiction. In the last version of *Saint Anthony*, the Sphinx's mouth is covered with lichen. 'I have meditated so much that I have nothing else to say,' it intones, and sinks into the sand, its riddle now pure aphasia. And in *Sentimental Education*, at a fancy-dress party, one of the guests is a young woman got up as 'the Sphinx'. This is what the great Egyptian statue has become: a fancy-dress costume (in a novel where all of history sometimes seems unreal to Frédéric, a form of playing out already-allotted parts). But 'the Sphinx' at the party, stoically swigging down the brandy, cheeks inflamed, starts coughing up blood; she is living it up because she is dying of consumption – and Frédéric, suddenly, feels sorry for her and tries to imagine her life.

Flaubert and Du Camp duly made the ascent of the Great Pyramid itself. Forty centuries (plus a few more years) looked down impassively on Gustave and Max as they struggled up the sides of the Great Pyramid. It was an exhausting business, as the stones that had to be climbed came up to their chests; they had to be hauled up by their Arab guides. For some reason Max seemed particularly eager to reach the summit. When Flaubert finally caught up with him – it was shortly before sunrise – he discovered a business card attached to the side of the Pyramid. It read *Hubert, frotteur* – the name of a floor-polisher. Flaubert was a little vexed: this was going to be *his* joke on Max. He had brought the card all the way from Rouen, in his folding hat; Max must have spotted it and stolen a march on him. The pinnacle of the Pyramid was no escape from the platitudes of Normandy. In fact, neither Gustave nor Max could claim priority for this moment of pyramidal high jinks: they had been preceded by a certain Buffard (address: 79, rue Saint-Martin, Paris), a wallpaper manufacturer, who had left his calling card before them. Farce preceded by fatuity (or vice versa): and yet, leaving one's name behind was what Egypt (and perhaps culture in general) was all about. A few years before, on a visit to Chillon, Flaubert had been irritated by the sight of the names written on the walls of the Byronically celebrated prison. In Alexandria he was greeted by the sight of the great column of Pompey; around its base, in letters three feet high, was the name 'Thomson of Sunderland'. This act of vandalism is of course enough to inspire anyone with apoplexy: but Pompey probably wouldn't have minded, since the pillar in question had nothing whatever to do with him, and its name is a misnomer. On a visit to Rome, Max had already written the words 'Gustave' and 'Maxime' on a pillar in the Temple of Fortune in the Forum. In the black rock of a cave at Gasmeh Shems, Flaubert found Egyptian hieroglyphs overlaid with Greek inscriptions: more palimpsests, no doubt placed there by the Thomsons of Sunderland, the Gustaves and the Maximes, of their day.

The view from the top of the Pyramid, in spite of Hubert and Buffard, was immense; and after breakfast they made the equally ritual descent into the pyramid's interior, crawling down the same corridors along which, Flaubert surmised, the huge royal coffins had been dragged. They reached the king's chamber; at the far end of it was a sarcophagus. It was empty.

The dry *pointillé* of Flaubert's notes on Sphinx and Pyramids, his relative indifference to their history, his abstention from interpretation, contrast with the attitudes of other French writers. Voltaire had never seen the Pyramids, but he knew what he thought of them: 'monuments of vanity and superstition', 'useless works' created by a 'people of slaves'. Chateaubriand, who travelled through Egypt in the autumn of 1806, did not have time to visit the Pyramids, but he rejected Voltaire's distaste for them, and admired them, from a distance, as a promise of immortality. (Unable to bear the thought of leaving no trace of his passage, 'I entrusted M. Caffre with the task of writing my name on those great tombs, as is the custom, at the earliest opportunity: one must fulfil all the little duties of a pious traveller.') Nerval, who had visited Cairo in 1842 (though his account of his travels, the *Voyage to the East*, was not published in book form until 1851), was equally wary of Voltaire's scepticism, but still felt that the Pyramids as they stood were lacking in a little something. Surely they could be put to better use than just being mute archaeological monuments? What about using their interior as a magnificent, and apt, setting for Mozart's *The Magic Flute*? 'Imagine the thunderous voice of Zarastro [sic] booming out from the depths of the hall of pharaohs, or the *Queen of the Night* making her appearance on the threshold of the so-called queen's chamber and launching her dazzling trills into its sombre vaults.' The melodies of the magic flute itself would echo down the long corridors, giving the quaking 'Papayeno' and the initiated Tamino the courage to confront the triple Anubis.

Nerval took his duties as a mediator between East and West seriously enough to 'marry' a local woman in Cairo. Flaubert was content with briefer couplings; but he too was eager to participate in local customs. He and Max were initiated into the circle of snake charmers. Snakes were placed around their necks and hands; incantations were recited over their heads; the charmers breathed into their mouths. 'The men who practise such culpable professions perform their vile impostures, as M. de Voltaire used to say, with remarkable skill,' Flaubert wrote to Bouilhet in a letter that he entitled, with mock pedantry, 'De saltatoribus', describing the male dancers (all the female dancers had been exiled to Upper Egypt) who performed for him and Du Camp: 'two really rather ugly fellows', but charming in their corruption, degradation, and femininity. Their eyes were painted with antimony, and they were dressed as women, their bellies, waists and upper buttocks being clad simply in a transparent black gauze. The lasciviousness of their sinuous dancing contrasted with the statuesque impassivity of their faces and their ceremonious bowings: hence the powerful effect of their performance. Their 'mahout', as Flaubert called their manager, skipped around them, kissing them on the stomach and the small of the back, uttering salacious little jokes to spice things up – though this was quite unnecessary. He later mused in a letter to Bouilhet that he would like to see Hasan come and dance again – this time, the (erotic) Dance of the Bee, for, when 'danced by a bardash...' Anyway, the dance, with the thin wail of the flute and the rattle of the castanets, gave him a migraine for the rest of the day.

He also visited the baths. He was alone; a murky light came in through the thick little panes of glass in the dome. There was hot water running everywhere. 'Stretched out like a calf, I lay thinking of many things; all my pores tranquilly dilated.' It was 'very voluptuous and sweetly melancholy' to bathe alone like this, in those dark halls, with only the naked Kellaks for company; 'they handle you and turn you over like embalmers laying you out for the tomb.' He once wrote, 'Lesbos is my country. I have its refinement and its languors.' And he told Sand he was 'of both sexes'.

Sometimes Flaubert, far from being the cool observer, was filled with exaltation. He saw the sun setting near Thebes; he had an intense sense of everything and nothing, and thanked God for his sensations. The desert was a relief from the hubbub of Alexandria and Cairo: he noted: 'Silence. Silence. Silence.' But the Orient and its dust made one realise the vanity of everything, even literature. He was also bored by the empty caves and the monotonous temples, one of which, at Edfu, was used as the communal latrine for the local village. Thoughts of literature started to take over; his travel notes – among the most elliptically vivid ever composed – are full of self-critical observations, as he ponders how to compose a scene, and wonders what kind of writing (if any) travel should produce. He was forever placating his mother by insisting that he was doing his homework (real research); and Maxime Du Camp, with the benefits of hindsight, tells us that Gustave was already obsessed by his future novel. After a three-hour climb to the summit of a mountain over-looking the Second Cataract with its black granite rocks spark-ling in the sunshine, Flaubert and Du Camp paused; this was the furthest south they would travel in Egypt; Flaubert shouted, 'Eureka! Eureka! I'm going to call her Madame Bovary!' repeat-ing the name several times (with a short 'o'). The story is beauti-ful; it may possibly be true.

Equally fine, however apocryphal, is another of Du Camp's *ben trovato* claims. He tells us that, as they returned from a camel trip into the desert, they ran out of water. Tormented by thirst, they almost started to hallucinate – and Gustave began to detail aloud all the delicious ice-cold drinks he had ever enjoyed. Maxime, his throat parched, felt like killing him. He wanted a real, not an imaginary, drink.

The two continued, in their sexual-tourist way, to avail them-selves of the local women. For Flaubert, Kuchuk Hanem, the *ghawazee* dancer of Esma, was the whore to Élisa Schlésinger's Madonna. We do not even know the real name of this celebrated courtesan of Upper Egypt: 'kuchuk hanem' means 'little lady' in Turkish – though she was originally from Damascus – and was probably the equivalent of a stage name. She was tall, and when Flaubert first saw her she was wearing pink trousers and a violet gauze. She smelled fresh ('sugared terebinth'), having just bathed. Her right upper incisor was blackened by decay – and 'a long line of writing in blue was tattooed upon her right arm'. Flaubert and Du Camp had sex with her almost on arrival. Later, she danced the Dance of the Bee (in which the woman pretends that a bee has invaded her clothing, and so has to divest herself of all her garments in rapid succession). The male musicians accompanying her were blindfolded. Flaubert admired her beautiful patellas. That night, she slept with Flaubert; she snored, coughed in her sleep; – and he covered her over with his cloak. In between their couplings, he drifted into melancholy reveries, wondering whether she would remember him. Then he started squashing the bedbugs on the chalk-white wall, leaving 'long black and red arabesques'. When he later showed Louise Colet his travel notes, she complained about the bedbugs: he retorted, in a letter, that their nauseating odour complemented the sandalwood dripping on Kuchuk's body, just as the lemon trees he later saw in Jaffa formed a 'complete poetry', a 'great synthesis' with the rotting corpses half-exposed in the cemetery there.

Several years later, during her own trip to Egypt, Louise made a point of trying to find out what had happened to Kuchuk Hanem – possibly out of jealousy, possibly out of its sister, curiosity. Gustave himself, inevitably, returned to visit Kuchuk Hanem on his way back up Egypt; she had been ill; everything was already more muted and melancholy.

From Egypt he brought back memories and metaphors. To Louise Colet he wrote: 'The way of living with serenity, in the open air, is to settle on a pyramid, any pyramid, so long as it's lofty and its base is solid. – Ah! It's not always much fun, and you're all alone, but you can derive some consolation from spitting down.' And, also to Louise: 'The mummies that one has in the heart never fall into dust and, when you poke your head through the air hole, you can see them down there, gazing at you open-eyed, immobile.'

The rest of Flaubert's expedition to the East was, after Egypt, a little anticlimactic. After three days in Jerusalem (which he thought was a den of thieves), he had experienced 'none of the emotions foreseen in advance': 'neither religious enthusiasm, nor arousal of the imagination, nor hatred of priests'. Once, in Bordeaux, he had touched the pages of Montaigne's *Essays* with the reverence due to 'a religious relic'; during his tour of Brittany, entering Chateaubriand's room in Combourg, he had piously removed his hat; in the Church of the Holy Sepulchre he felt emptier than an empty barrel. Whose fault was it, he asked. The priests'? His own? Or 'Yours' (i.e. God's)? He saw the Wailing Wall, and later turned it into a figure of his own decrepitude: 'I am like the Temple of Solomon, I cannot be rebuilt.' But Bethlehem was beautiful: 'it sings of mystic joy'.

In Beirut, he may have picked up syphilis from a fourteen-year-old Maronite boy. (The exact details of how such illnesses are contracted sometimes take centuries to determine.) He made the ascent of Mount Carmel. Near Damascus, a group of lepers were living in isolation on a farm. The nose of one woman' eaten away; her fingers were green tatters.

In Istanbul, he had dinner with the consul, General Aupick and his wife, who asked tentatively whether Flaubert had come across her son; he was a writer, his name was Charles Baudelaire. During his stay here, Flaubert also heard of the death of Balzac. There was a performance of *Lucia di Lammermoor*.

His first sight of Athens, from the decks of the *Mentor*, filled him with happiness. He picked up two pieces of marble from the Acropolis, as souvenirs for Croisset. At Thermopylae, he and Du Camp read Plutarch's account of the Three Hundred. Flaubert thought it would make 'a splendid story'. In Patras he wrote a prose poem about tits.

In Italy he saw Naples and did not die – but he *was* almost drowned while swimming off the isle of Capri. He was offered girls of ten to sleep with – but he had a chancre. He climbed Vesuvius. He shared Gibbon's contempt for the way Christianity had appropriated and spoiled Rome, and found St Peter's frigid and pompous: 'I prefer Greek, I prefer gothic, I prefer the little mosque with its minaret soaring into the air like a great cry', he wrote to Bouilhet. But he did feel a grudging respect for the Popes, their power and their artistic taste. *'Quels messieurs!'* He relapsed into the usual clichés of the Grand Tour: in the Sistine, he reflected that Michelangelo was 'a Shakespearean Homer, a mixture of antiquity and the Middle Ages, *je ne sais quoi*'. He fell in love with Murillo's *Virgin* in the Corsini gallery: her eyes hovered in front of him like dancing lanterns.

Then he was back in Croisset, writing. In a letter dated 'Saturday evening' (it was 20th September 1851) he told Colet, 'Yesterday evening I began my novel. I am starting to see difficulties of style that fill me with horror. It's no easy business, being simple. I'm afraid of relapsing into Paul de Kock or of producing Chateaubrianised Balzac.' This was *Madame Bovary*.

Aesthetics at midnight

The aesthetic tenet of impersonality (the idea that the work of art should be independent of its creator's life) is one that he hammered out in the rather personal form of love letters to Louise Colet, written night after night, after days composing *Madame Bovary*. He never uttered it as a public programmatic statement. Living through the early days of the avant-garde, in which it was becoming increasingly incumbent on the artist to found a school, produce a programme, or issue a manifesto, Flaubert became increasingly aloof. The only aesthetic he produced was an owl of Minerva that took flight after the day's work was done; it was often part of a process of self-definition in which his addressee (especially Louise Colet or George Sand) was his opposite. Thus his own aesthetic – masculine, concise, vigorous, plotted, 'heartless' – was defined *as against* the spontaneous and fluent Colet or the humanitarian sympathies of Sand, even though he admired the latter's work. Louise Colet sent him her poetry to comment on and correct as he was writing *Madame Bovary* (and correct it he did, although he was not a poet, with considerable conscientiousness). His was an aesthetics *ad hominem* (or *contra mulierem*). He disdained to deliver his views on art to a public hungry for pronouncements on these issues (as he showed, satirically, in the art-jargonising painter Pellerin, in *Sentimental Education*). This was the great age of prefaces: Hugo, Gautier, the Goncourts, all set out their aims and objectives in this way. Flaubert once mused that he might 'puke up a little preface' one day – but only to introduce a work (the *Dictionary of Received Ideas*) in which he would lambast the human desire for quick fixes of precisely this prefatorial kind. In 1871 he rebuked Zola for, as it were, giving the game away: Zola had published a clarion call of a preface to the second edition of *Thérèse Raquin*. When, towards the end of Flaubert's life, everyone was taking up positions, and curious to discover where he stood in the field of cultural production, he shrugged. 'All dogmatism exasperates me', he wrote, dogmatically, exasperatingly. Realism? He wrote *Madame Bovary* out of hatred for it (just as he wrote, more generally, out of hatred for reality). Naturalism? 'Me no *comprenez*,' he pidgined; too many coarse words – and why on earth did Zola have to write the same way his workers and peasants spoke? Still, he admired *L'Assommoir*, and personal reservations did not always prevent him from giving considerable encouragement to fellow writers – as Edmond de Goncourt commented at the unveiling of the Flaubert memorial, referring to Zola, Daudet, Maupassant, and himself, all present to remember the cantankerous and affectionate Master who had vouchsafed to their endeavours, among the growls of dissent, the odd grunt of solidarity and even enthusiasm. As for impressionism, or symbolism... He gave an unGallic shrug. Never has such a major French writer taken ideas so seriously (his reading – on history, on politics, on philosophy – was staggering: just for the sake of a few details in *Saint Anthony* he ploughed his way through Plotinus' complete *Enneads* – which he loathed) while being so resolutely anti-intellectual. He loved – or hated – ideas too much to choose between them. Any idea that had ever been entertained was still alive, and could spiral back into view. But as for discussing them in public... Ideas were like bodily fluids, to be exchanged between consenting adults in private. If ideas darkened the pages of a novel, it was to be as mere bric-à-brac, on a par with a piece of furniture or an item of clothing: if his last novel, *Bouvard and Pécuchet*, is a novel of ideas, it is only in order to satirise as many of them as possible, to play with the idea that all ideas are simply received – or even that there is something wrong with ideas as such, especially when they become slogans, mere results. If he had an idea, it was Literature. He sometimes wrote about this in tones of wistful longing: he had such an idea of prose (such an idea – you have no idea!) that he doubted whether it was realisable. All writing stood under the baleful judgement of Writing. Balzac would have been a great man if only he'd been able to... write. But Flaubert derived little sense of satisfaction even from the stylistic achievement of his own works: once the writing was done and he had killed off the possibility of any improvement by having it published, he distanced himself from the monument he had so laboriously erected, finding fault with it, looking askance at contemporaries who praised it. Literature, a savage god, glared down at him from a serene, ironically blue sky; he would never appease it. Manifestoes and movements were evasions of its cruel demands; he would never join in the games played by the schools, with all their -isms; the only -ist he cared to be was an artist: as much of a *position* as the others, though he preferred to think it was above such things.

Who were his models? 'Homer, Rabelais, Michelangelo, Shakespeare, Goethe seem to me to be pitiless.' (Interestingly, none of these were essentially novelists: the only novelist he admitted to his pantheon was Cervantes.) All of them were 'bottomless, infinite, multiple. Through little chinks you can glimpse precipices; there's blackness down there, vertigo. And yet something strangely gentle hovers over it all! It's the gleam of the light, the smiling of the sun, and it's calm! it's calm! And it's strong!' This seems like a description of a nervous attack (the darkness, the depths, the vortex) redeemed by something vague and lofty floating above.

He had read the *Odyssey* as he travelled down the Nile; his love of Shakespeare (*Timon of Athens*, with its misanthropic hero; *Pericles*; *Macbeth*...) remained constant, even though his grasp of the language was uncertain. Sartre points out that Flaubert seems to have misunderstood the plot of *King Lear* (Gustave thinks that Edgar is really mad), and 'dreams' himself into the play, as a useless 'bastard' son, a bit like Edmund – Sartre focuses intensely on Gustave's sense that his parents both preferred his older brother Achille and that he, Gustave, had been cheated of his birthright. Flaubert would later take English lessons from Miss Juliet Herbert, his niece Caroline's tutor between 1855 and 1857; he found her an attractive woman (he compared her bosom with the glacis of a fortress), and confessed in a letter that only with an effort did he refrain from pinching her bottom as they climbed the staircase. But he visited her in England in 1865 and they continued to meet sporadically. It was observed that he was making considerable progress with his English.

Madame Bovary

This is a novel in which escape (the attempt to transcend the given) is imposed as a duty, but every escape route is systematically blocked. All the characters are allowed to do is to paint the bars of their cage. It is not even permissible to say that the life portrayed here is dull and provincial, since, seen the right way (but by whom? 'For something to be interesting, you just need to look at it for a long time') it can be a thing of strange, mesmeric beauty. What disconcerted Flaubert's earliest readers was the way the text seemed to be tempting them into opinions (Emma is too imaginative and educated for her own good; Bournisien is much more of an imbecile than most country priests; Homais is a self-satisfied spinner of platitudes; Charles is a dull clodhopper) which the text not only refuses to endorse, but scrutinises quizzically – not least because most of Flaubert's characters are always passing judgement on each other ('how stupid!' says Homais; 'what a load of nonsense!' thinks Rodolphe), so that to pass judgement immediately makes the reader, potentially, one of Flaubert's characters. All judgements stand under judgement. Charles stares at his medical books with incomprehension. Gustave stared at his law books in catatonic stupor. Charles fails his first university exams. So did Gustave. 'So what?' it is tempting to think: Flaubert's world comprises many shades of grey, and it is foolish for pots to call kettles black. There is a disjunction between the imprecise vagueness of judgement on the one hand, and the exactitude of the objects described on the other. This is because, for Flaubert, human beings and the objects around them suffuse each other: psychology simply is a matter of objects. For this reason, Lukács correctly pointed out that Flaubert did not need to analyse or evaluate his characters: the 'atmosphere' of the novel was quite enough. Sometimes the characters seem to have walk-on parts in a world of things, of animals, vegetables and minerals that are all more alive than the human beings. The punctuation enjoys adventures as exciting as Emma's – the italics which sometimes pinpoint a cliché or a bit of free indirect discourse, but which sometimes serve merely to make the reader stir uneasily; the typical semi-colon followed by a dash as if the text were winking at us, or weeping ; – and commas, dashes, colons, all yawn and stretch as they hover over the world, waiting to puncture the text with a hiatus, a dehiscence. A whispered prompt of Homais to his wife as he tries to impress the surgeon (Emma is dying, but first things first...) has three exclamation marks lavished on it. In fact, whenever Homais appears, the text really starts to enjoy itself. How he handles the French language, and the other languages which he half-knows! Bits of Latin ('*Saccharum*, doctor?') or English ('*That is the question!*', which he's read in the newspaper, or the single word '*Yes*', which he uses to Léon, à propos of nothing in particular). Pretentious? '*Homais sum, nihil humanum...*'

The first of six instalments of Flaubert's novel appeared in the *Revue de Paris* on 1st October 1856. Readers' letters were soon flooding in, complaining of immorality, calling the work 'a calumny on the French nation', as Du Camp reported. Flaubert was rehearsing Louis Bouilhet's play at the Odéon theatre. Its first night was a great success, and a banquet was organised to celebrate. But at the beginning of November, Du Camp was visited by a friend, who had it on the highest authority that the *Revue de Paris* was going to be prosecuted. The publication was already under suspicion because it had published writers who had been active under the Second Republic and might be considered dissident towards the Empire. Du Camp advised cuts, notably the scene (itself already alluded to, rather than shown) between Emma and Léon in the carriage trundling round Rouen and environs. Flaubert refused, but was eventually forced to accept the suppression of this scene – but he insisted that the readers be informed his novel had been mutilated. The cut (which paradoxically drew attention to what was never explicitly there in the first place) was not enough to prevent the trial for immorality and irreligion that ensued.

The trial

In January 1857, Flaubert was waiting from one minute to the next for the *papier timbré* that would inform him which day he was 'to sit (for the crime of having written in French) on the bench with swindlers and pederasts'. The hearing was fixed for Saturday 24th January, but for a while, when further details were not forthcoming, Flaubert thought the affair might blow over. One of his powerful protectors was apparently so enraged at the prospect of a trial that he threatened to go and smash the windows in the Tuileries. But the *papier timbré* finally arrived, and Flaubert was soon collecting incriminating evidence from the classics for his defence lawyer, Sénard. He requested a friend to ask the Abbé Constant for 'as many lubricious passages as possible from church authors, particularly the moderns'. He intended to publish a *Mémoire* in his own defence; the court forbade it. But he was pessimistic about the outcome. The evening before the trial, he wrote to Gautier to pull strings with the highest authorities.

His prosecutor, Pinard, initially used the technique of close reading to incriminate the 'lascivious colour' of the book. He realised that concentrating on excerpts would necessarily be tendentious: but he insisted that he had not omitted a single scene in his overview, and his main point was that Emma Bovary was out of control. 'Who can condemn this woman in the book? Nobody.' (Did any member of the jury show a flicker of recognition at these words?) All her potential critics – even the Abbé Bournisien – were shown as derisory. Only by taking up a standpoint outside the novel, that of Christian morality, could Emma (and thus the novel) be indicted.

Sénard, for the defence, used a more biographical-historical approach. M. Flaubert, he tells the jury, is the worthy son of a decent father; his whole family is entirely respectable. He has taken the trouble to see the world: like Ulysses, *'mores multorum vidit et urbes'*. He has studied law. He has the support of the very eminent poet Lamartine. And as for the suggestive passages quoted – entirely out of context – by the prosecution, our classical writers wrote much worse things! Read Rousseau, read Montesquieu, read Mérimée, read Chénier, read Sainte-Beuve! The deathbed scene in which Emma kisses the crucifix with 'the biggest kiss of love she had ever given' does indeed register the interweaving of erotic and religious impulses – but we find this, too, in the writings of mystics and bishops: read St Teresa, read Fénelon, that swan of Cambrai, read Bossuet, that pillar of the church! The scene of extreme unction which the prosecution found so indecent (Flaubert had paraphrased, instead of correctly quoting, the sacred words) was based closely on a book about the catechism lent to Flaubert by one of his friends, a 'venerable ecclesiastic' – a book that had been approved by their Lordships the Bishops and Archbishops of Le Mans, of Tours, of Bordeaux, of Cologne, etc. So to attack the incriminated passage in Flaubert is to attack the Church herself. Sénard wound up by pointing out that *Madame Bovary* was a first novel, and had taken two or three years of incessant work to produce (a considerable understatement).

Thus Pinard seems to rely on an immanent critique which then reveals itself to be based on judgements taken from outside the text, while Sénard begins by placing the novel in a personal, historical and cultural context, only to say, at the end, that its achievement is stylistic. Perhaps one day, like Homais and the Abbé Bournisien arguing over Emma's dead body, they might even have agreed?

Flaubert and his publishers were acquitted with a mere rap on the knuckles: the book was coherent, but many passages were in bad taste: what is an art that does not follow rules?

In this way men talked in worried tones about absent, wayward, and dead women, and pondered on the knotted tangle of religion, sexuality, and literary technique. A novel that indicts novels had been indicted for having done so in a way that was (and still is) deeply disturbing.

A young Russian novelist (and future indicter of novels) was in Paris at the time. Count Lev Nikolayevich Tolstoy took little notice, preferring to fret over the tasteless tomb of Napoleon (*that Antichrist!*) in the Invalides.

In September 1873, Flaubert said that he was happy for the details of the trial to be published in a new edition of *Madame Bovary*.

Apart from being put on trial for his novel, Flaubert was also subjected to the tender mercies of the critics.

The journal *Réalisme* attacked the novel harshly for being too well written. Sainte-Beuve thought the novel had 'a severe and pitiless truth'. It was unfair for the novel to have been put on trial; – and yet, there were perhaps certain *risqué* passages where the novelist might have been just a little more cautious… Flaubert should have known he was going to be read by the French – who have such dirty minds. For Barbey d'Aurevilley, Flaubert was a story-telling machine, a 'man of marble' who had written *Madame Bovary* with a 'pen of stone' that was as cutting as 'the knife of savages'; he looked at everything through a microscope; he was 'an entomologist of style who would describe elephants in the same way as insects'. George Sand concurred with Emma Bovary that Emma Bovary was the only intelligent person in this 'gathering of cretins'. Baudelaire, finally, thought that Flaubert had put the most solemn and decisive words into the mouths of the greatest imbeciles in the most stupid of environments (the French provinces); he had proved that all subjects, even the dullest of all (adultery), could be handled well with sufficient analysis, logic, and stylistic exactitude; and he had undergone a sex change. By turning himself into a woman, he had made Emma into a man – man at his most energetic and ambitious, and at his dreamiest, too. For Emma is not only a man, she is a dandy; not just a hysteric, but a combination of calculation and reverie – a 'perfect being'. She is an intellectual woman, far removed from 'pure animal', yet she is also Pasiphae; she bestrides her narrow world like a colossus, she is 'Caesar in Carpentras'. A century later, Sartre would agree: for all his impersonality, Flaubert had produced, in *Madame Bovary*, a disguised autobiography.

In later life, Flaubert grew to detest the way that (as Barbey d'Aurevilley kept sneeringly insinuating) he was a one-book man – the book being *Madame Bovary*. He dreamed of winning a fortune so that he could buy back all the copies and pulp it. He started to find in it examples of grammatical *gaucherie* and even involuntary *bêtise*. On 3rd March 1862, the Goncourt diary noted that Flaubert was consumed by remorse; his life was poisoned, he would go to an early grave: he had placed two genitives in *Madame Bovary* one after the other: *'une couronne de fleurs d'oranger'*! He had tried to avoid it, but in vain. In fact, in the novel as we have it, this double genitive is not there: the text simply reads *'une couronne d'orangers'*, describing the wreath of orange flowers in the hair of Lucia di Lammermoor. An an-gelic copy-editor evidently spotted the mistake, and silently corrected it.

The novel and its characters have had a long afterlife. There have been at least six reincarnations of Emma, as well as three versions of her orphaned daughter Berthe, a Madame Homais, and two versions of the story which both 'focalise' the narrative through the eyes of Charles Bovary. One of these, Antoine Billot's 2006 novel *Monsieur Bovary* (Laura Grimaldi had produced a novel under the same name in 1995), is based on extracts from Charles's diary (Charles – keeping a diary?), interwoven with a third-person narrative comprising the ten notebooks written by a certain B. (Billot?) found near the town of Ry, in Normandy. Before meeting Emma, Charles has already experienced romantic love for a young woman called 'Marie' (a common enough name, but also that of the heroine of *November*); he is not really stupid, merely pretending; – and, far from being the unobservant husband of Flaubert's novel, he has knowingly connived at and indeed organised his wife's affairs, for his own perverse pleasures. Nabokov had already wondered whether a sturdy young man like Charles would really snore his nights away, unaware that his young wife was slipping out of bed to meet Rodolphe in the arbour; Billot takes things a stage further, turning cuckold into knowing pimp. In *Contre-enquête sur la mort d'Emma Bovary* by Philippe Doumenc, we are reminded that a single dose of arsenic is rarely fatal. Canivet discovers traces of bruising, Larivière hears the dying Emma murmuring 'murder, not suicide...'

The novel sometimes falls victim to the knowingness that often afflicts Flaubertians (been there, done that): we all know about his 'little woman' with fire and then arsenic in her belly, and about the fatuities of life in Dullsville or Yonville. It is interesting to see how it has been received in other cultures. The first translations into Chinese (from 1925 onwards) found themselves obliged to put in anthropological footnotes explaining that when Emma's father sees the black cloth hanging outside the Bovary house he realises she is dead, because, in the West, black is associated with mourning. Chinese readers were told not to expect a classical tale of secret loves between refined scholars and beautiful ladies. The problems of translation and cultural reference led to puzzlement over some scenes: in one Mandarin version, the peasants at Emma's wedding are said to be applying onion skins to their shaving cuts; Emma's 'mania for prawns' is interpreted as a sign of 'stubbornness'; the exotic 'piano' is transliterated as an incomprehensible '*pi ya le*', and Léon's room overlooking the town square becomes 'a little hut on the second floor, facing the *pu la si* [*la place*]'. The copious but homely fare served at Emma's wedding (veal, chicken, suckling pig and mutton) might have struck many Chinese readers in the 1920s as an extraordinarily lavish feast. One translator, Li Jianwu, visited Rouen in the 1930s; he saw Loulou, the stuffed parrot of 'A Simple Heart', and was filled by melancholy when he realised that Flaubert's desk had been sold by his niece Caroline. It was Li Jianwu who found a suitable Chinese idiom to describe Emma's marriage to Charles: 'a beautiful phoenix following a raven'. Emma and Charles thus became honorary citizens of the Middle Kingdom.

The book continued, and continues, to have political reson-ances. In the 1920s, Chinese women were starting to become critically aware of their traditional roles: Emma was held up as a model, or, more often, a dreadful warning. A recent trans-lation into Farsi bears a warning on its cover: this is a novel in which indulging in fashionable cravings by being a *sodahee*, a fantasist, a passionate woman, is as dangerous as setting fire to your house.

There have been several films, some of them very fine: Renoir, Minnelli, Chabrol (with a deliciously frigid-lascivious Isabelle Huppert, and, for some reason, a parrot in Charles's consulting room). One produced at the tail-end of the swing-ing sixties is known in Italian as *I Peccati di Madame Bovary* (*The Sins of Madame Bovary*), in German as *Die Nackte Bovary* (*The Naked Bovary Woman*), and in the United Kingdom as *Play the Game or Leave the Bed*. A voluptuous Emma with a superb embonpoint plays the piano rather well, and decides not to commit suicide. In *Maya Memsaab*, Bollywood conventions are deployed with great effect: the 'Charles' figure arrives at Maya's (Emma's) palatial dwelling on a bike (not quite like the prince of her dreams, but still…); they dance and sing; unusually for such a film, the tragedy of the ending is not avoided. The result is a hauntingly different take on a European classic.

Paris life

The scandal, and then the success, of *Madame Bovary* gave Flaubert an entrée to the salons of Paris, where he would now winter, enjoying the company of the literati, selectively. He sallied out in his frock coat, feeling as if he were 'in disguise'. Magny's restaurant on the Left Bank, where Sainte-Beuve had in late 1862 initiated his series of dinners, every other Saturday, for writers and scholars, was the scene of some of Flaubert's most eloquent *gueulades*, as well as the place where he met Turgenev, who became a close friend (Turgenev was to translate Flaubert's 'St Julian' and 'Herodias' into Russian). Here cultural deities (Voltaire, Rousseau) were feted or mocked; advanced thinking was fostered (there was a distinctly anti-clerical hue to many of the conversations), and guests occasionally threw up out of the window. Other habitués of these dinners included the Goncourt brothers (Edmond enjoyed the occasions but also found them 'a bloody pain'); their diaries contain many closely observed, cattily fraternal, sceptically respectful vignettes of Flaubert holding forth: more of a bull than a bear, at least on 18th January 1864 – with his inflamed face, his bellowing voice, his swollen eyes, declaring that 'beauty is not erotic'. On other occasions, Flaubert would dance 'The Idiot of the Salons', in which he capered about with his collar turned up and his scant hair on end.

Flaubert would eventually start receiving on a Sunday, between one and seven in the evening, in his own fifth-floor apartment. According to Maupassant, as soon as the first visitor was announced, he would throw a light red silk cover over the table on which lay his scattered pages, covered with his writing, and his inkwell and pens – for these were 'as sacred to him as the ritual objects are for a priest'. Here he was visited by Henry James, who observed him at full flow in his 'long colloquial dressing-gown'.

Having been put on trial by the Second Empire, he was now enfolded within its capacious cultural embrace. Princess Mathilde, the niece of Napoleon Bonaparte and cousin of Napoleon III, presided over gatherings of the great (and the good) at the imperial court of Compiègne, in the Tuileries and at the Palais-Royal. Flaubert was summoned to attend for the first time in June 1867. He developed a tender attachment to the Princess; indeed, in the Palais-Royal he was observed sitting on the steps of the throne flirting with her. According to the Goncourts, who also attended many of these meetings of the imperial intelligentsia, the Princess was not above calling them all 'bloody pigs!' The Goncourts found that, in the Princess's salons, Flaubert always had better stories to tell than everyone else; he was gross, domineering, a hectoring bully. 'So much nervous tension, so much pugnacious violence emanates from Flaubert that the circles in which he finds himself soon become stormy, and everyone is overcome by a certain aggressiveness.' But everyday contact made him really affectionate, with his child-like laugh.

Flaubert was an eternal corrector: the *Sottisier* on which he worked, sporadically, all his life was to include choice mistakes, errors of fact and tact, gathered from even the best writers: an assembly of out-takes and bloopers. Literature: *castigavit et emendavit* G. Flaubert... He even tried to correct a piece the Princess had written about her beloved dead dog Didi. Even at court, he remained his own man. He protested indignantly against gossip that he had waved the satirical, anti-Empire magazine *La Lanterne* about at Compiègne; but he did, according to Du Camp, defend the self-exiled Victor Hugo in front of the Empress, and even threatened to recite some of *Les Châtiments*, Hugo's magnificent verse invective against the man he also dubbed *Napoléon le Petit*. The subject of the conversation was quickly changed.

Salammbô

On the warm night of 23rd April 1858, Flaubert wrote to Bouilhet from the ship *Tanit* that was sailing to Tunisia, the coast of which was distantly visible through the sea-mist. The sea was 'as flat as a lake of oil', the Captain was next to him smoking his pipe, the deck was covered with Arab pilgrims en route for Mecca, wrapped in their white burnouses, their faces veiled, their feet bare: 'they look like corpses in their shrouds'. When he landed, he saw the vultures wheeling in the sky. It was at Philippeville, 'in a garden full of rose trees in flower', as the waves were plashing against the shore and the negro gardener was walking off to fetch a watering-can, that the idea of how to write the story of the city of Carthage during the Mercenary War again sprang to his mind. In the rose garden there was a Roman mosaic of two women, one sitting on a horse, the other on a sea-monster. The gardener came back; he poured the water from the watering-can in front of Flaubert 'to make the lovely colours of the mosaic come alive again'. Mosaic, as he knew, was an art whose secret had been lost: perhaps he could rediscover it. Musing on the beach, he saw a young woman striding along the sand, wearing purple boots with a high ankle binding. He started.

He wrote to his niece Caroline to tell her that he had seen flocks of flamingos flying up from the Lake of Tunis; it was so pretty when you took a shot at them, they flew away in clouds of pink and black. On the way to Utica he had lain awake in a Bedouin *douar*, between 'two walls of cow dung, amid the dogs and poultry', listening to the howling of the jackals. The next morning he had gone on a scorpion hunt, and with his whip killed a metre-long snake that was winding itself round the legs of his horse.

Meanwhile, he dreamed among the ruins; and in the note-book he kept during his expedition to Carthage, he wrote a prayer. 'May all the energies of nature which I have breathed in penetrate me, and may they be breathed out into my work. Come to me, powers of creative emotion! To me, resurrection of the past, to me, to me! Through the Beautiful, something living and true must *also* be made. Have pity on my willpower, God of souls! Give me Strength and Hope!'

On 20th June 1858, on his return to Croisset, he wrote to tell Ernest Feydeau: '*Carthage* needs to be done all over again – or rather, just done. *I'm demolishing everything*. It was absurd! Impossible! Wrong!' *Delenda est Carthago*. But only in order to be rebuilt, and this time *with feeling*. 'I think I'm going to get the right tone. I'm starting to understand my characters and to take an interest in them.'

He had undertaken the writing of what he at first called *Carthage* as an escape route from the modern world to which he had bound himself in *Madame Bovary*. This was not a self-imposed *pensum* – this was what he *really* wanted to write; he would perhaps rediscover the brio and facility of his *oeuvres de jeunesse*. No more Yonville – it was time to 'put on the tragic buskin', to 'let roar – always good for the health!' But soon he was venting his epistolary lamentations as before. 'I'm having real problems with Carthage!' His real worry was 'the psycho-logical part', and the religious aspect; and the 'local colour' seemed so irrelevant...

He sought inspiration, as ever, in massive feats of ingestion, devouring learned tomes as Moloch devoured children, in the hope that fructifying rain would fall. By 26th July 1857 he had swallowed some hundred volumes on Carthage; it took him a

fortnight to work his way through Cahen's Talmudic comment-
aries on the Bible (he made notes on Cahen's notes). Another
fortnight's research, he told Jules Duplan, and then a week's
intense 'reverie', and then he could set sail in his trireme. (Strictly
speaking, a quinquereme would have been more appropriate.)
'It's not that I'm the least bit *inspired*, but I want to see it. It's
a kind of curiosity and, as you might say, a lubricious desire without an erection.' Perhaps the ruins would not rise? Day after
day he struggled to *see* what he was writing about, for the idea
to flower in all its colour. In November he felt he had come to
a dead end; he had not carried the book in his belly for long
enough; he could not write a word. His Punic ambitions had
been punished (a grim pun that seems to echo in many of his
cries of distress in this period). Over the winter months of 1857–8
he continued, under the dark skies of Croisset, to be tormented
by the sterile wastes of desert sand several hundred miles and
two millennia away. In January, staring open-mouthed at his pile
of blackened notes, he decided that he needed the field trip we
have already accompanied him on. He came back, and plunged
into a description of the city's inhabitants – their 'clothes,
government, religion, finances and trade, etc.' His regime of
research often kept him busy from eight in the morning until
dusk, taking notes in Paris libraries, reading Procopius, Polybius,
Strabo, Xenophon. But one thing he could not consult was
Carthaginian literature: a whole mentality had to be summoned
back into existence from largely hostile accounts. He was doing
something unprecedented: 'giving people a language in which
they never thought!' Building Carthage in his mind was a laborious
and dangerous process. The 'topographic and pictorial description of the city' gave him a frisson of joy mingled with anxiety:
'*I am in a labyrinth.*' The hot yellow sun of Libya was crossed out
again and again in furious black ink. It was going to kill him. And
yet, by late December, he was starting to enjoy himself. 'Finally
the thing is standing erect [...] even though I've had to whip
myself up and manustuprate myself.' Like Mâtho and Spendius

stealing into the city via its aqueduct, he had to hold his breath, uncertain where he would surface; he carried 'two entire armies on his shoulders, 30 thousand men on the one side, eleven thousand on the other, not to mention the elephants with their elephantarchs, camp followers, bags and baggage!' While depicting acts of cannibalism, he was eating himself up with anxiety: so many repetitions, so much monotony in the shape of the sentences... and *too many soldiers*. But that was historically accurate. And yet historical accuracy could be boring...

He took time off from the antinomies of History and Art by summoning the Goncourts to Croisset. 'Here's the programme: (1) I'll start howling at 4 o'clock on the dot. – So turn up at around 3. (2) At 7, oriental dinner. You'll be served with human flesh, bourgeois brains and tigress clitorises sautéed in rhinoceros butter. (3) After coffee, the Punic bellowing will resume until the listeners snuff it. Does that suit you?' (But where was he to find *bourgeois brains*?) After this feast, fortified by encouragement from Louis Bouilhet (who told him 'remember that the *Iliad* [too] is simply a series of similar combats, and almost identical situations'), but still 'filled with gloom and bitterness', he sat down before Carthage, in mid-July of 1861, to invest the city with *ballistae* and other catapults. He lived like a priest, his existence was 'monotonous, paltry and washed-out' – all the drama, grandeur, and colour were in the Carthage of his imagination. He told the Goncourts that on one occasion he spent thirty-eight hours in succession on his book; at table he no longer had the strength to lift the jug and pour himself a drink. Soon, he'd had it up to here with the art of ancient war: he was puking up catapults, had *tollenones* up his arse, and was pissing scorpions. 'La Bovary's poisoning made me throw up in my chamber pot. The assault on Carthage is making my arms stiff. – And yet this is the most agreeable of professions!'

As he approached the end, he uttered a remark noted in the Goncourts' *Diary*. 'It's finished; I have only a dozen sentences to write, but I have all the cadences [*chutes de phrases*] worked out!' Rhythm was a fact as insistent as the details of war machines.

Publication of the novel met with acclaim, dismay, boredom, and the slings and arrows of outraged scholarship. He was attacked for having invented his sources (unless – as one reviewer, Anatole Claveau, sniffily remarked – Flaubert had access to materials that were 'visible to himself alone'). The epigraphist Guillaume Froehner pointed out that Flaubert incorrectly put the word 'stèle' in the feminine. The battle of Carthage became a battle of the books. *Froehner*: Your references to precious stones are all wrong. *Flaubert*: They are quite correct! Read Theophrastus! Read Pliny and Athenaeus! *Froehner*: How can you possibly claim that your nomads ate lice and monkeys? *Flaubert*: read Herodotus' *History*!

One of the more agreeable reactions led to a friendship that brought considerable cheer to Flaubert's life. George Sand wrote a very positive review of *Salammbô* in *La Presse* of 27th January 1863. She praised him for having the leisure to devote years to such an off-beat subject and to treat it in such an experimental way. The novel was 'strange and hypnotic', full of 'darkness and shards of light'. He had enabled her to travel back to a time of atrocities, to an 'African Babylon', with its 'cannibal poetry': something like Dante's *Inferno*. In 1852, Flaubert had written 'Every day, I read George Sand and regularly wax indignant for a good quarter of an hour': but he also enjoyed her novels, less guarded and uptight than his own; and at the Magny dinner where they met for the first time, in February 1866, he was the guest with whom she instinctively struck up the closest rapport.

Sainte-Beuve wrote a severe, erudite critique of the novel (in which he claimed, firstly that Flaubert had got many of his facts wrong, and secondly that this hardly mattered – how could anyone be so interested in such a byway of history?). Flaubert wrote an equally detailed rejoinder, catapulting libraries full of antiquarian books at his opponent. He also defended himself against the charge that he took a sadistic delight in the barbarity shown in the *bellum inexpiabile*. 'I believe I was less harsh towards humanity in *Salammbô* than in *Madame Bovary*. It seems to me that there is something inherently moral about the love that drew me towards extinct religions and peoples.' Flaubert could not lose: if attacked on the subject of historical accuracy, he could either counter-attack with his own immense dossier of facts, or retire into the aesthetic (he had merely written the novel to create the impression of the colour scarlet; in any case, the aim of art, even an art as apparently realistic as his own, was simply to create 'a vague exaltation').

In writing *Salammbô*, Flaubert was – as usual – obsessed by the visual. But vivid mental imagery was the exact opposite of a painting or drawing: he resented any idea of illustrated editions of his work – they would 'fix' the image, destroy the 'character of generality' in which the mental image alone could bathe, for 'a written woman makes you dream of a thousand women'. So no illustrations: the very idea, which his publisher Lévy insistently dangled before him, threw him into a '*phrenzy*', a fury '*impossible to describe*'. Where was the wretch who would paint Hannibal's portrait – or even draw a Carthaginian chair? 'It was hardly worth the effort of employing so much art so as to deliberately to leave everything vague, if some lout was going to come along and demolish my dream with his inept precision.' But he was intrigued by the idea that *Salammbô* might be turned into an opera, especially with Verdi as composer: Gautier was given the task of writing a libretto; he dallied over it for many months, and never finished it.

At the Imperial court, there was talk of basing some fancy-dress costumes on Salammbô's magnificent apparel. Did no one remember that Carthage had been a doomed empire and whisper *Sic transit*?

The influence of *Salammbô* has often been pictorial, musical and cinematic. In many canvases, a naked oriental woman gazes languidly into the shadows as a snake coils round her hips and breasts, as in Salammbô's scene with a serpent, depicted in chapter ten. The novel was translated into Russian within a year of its French publication; Modest Mussorgsky, who shared a flat in St Petersburg with a group of five other young Russian intellectuals, greeted it with enthusiasm. They read it to each other in the evenings – and Mussorgsky quickly started work on an opera called *Salammbô*, to his own libretto based on Flaubert; he abandoned it in 1866, but several of its main themes were recycled in his epic study of omens, murder, civil war and tyranny, *Boris Godunov*. (Mâtho, imprisoned in the citadel of Carthage before his death, is given an *arioso* that was transmuted into Boris's dying delirium.) Six scenes of the score were orchestrated by Zoltán Peskó, at the suggestion of Luigi Nono; it is a fascinating triangulation of Russian, French, and 'Oriental' themes, occupying a musical world somewhere between the deserts of Libya (as imagined largely from Normandy) and the steppes of Old Muscovy (with pianos, harps and glockenspiels signifying an ancient, barbaric, and oriental otherness). When the Bastille opera house reopened in 2000, the first performance was of a new opera by Philippe Fénélon, called *Salammbô*, with percussion and woodwind timbres predominating. In *Citizen Kane*, Charles Foster Kane promotes an opera on the same subject specifically to show off his wife's star qualities as a singer – we hear her rendering 'Salaambo's Aria' (actually composed by Bernard Herrmann). A milestone in the development of silent cinema was the Italian film *Cabiria*, directed by Giovanni Pastrone and released in 1914, just after a war between Italy and Turkey in which Italy had conquered the Ottoman provinces of Cyrenaica and Tripolitania, in which the site of Carthage was situated, and at the beginning of a slugfest that would be as lumberingly bloody and monotonous as the Mercenary War. The intertitles were written by Gabriele D'Annunzio. Cabiria is a Sicilian girl who is captured by Phoenician pirates, taken across the great sea swell, and sold into slavery in Carthage, where she is doomed to be sacrificed in the fires of Moloch. This is really the only link to Flaubert's novel (and the film draws equally on Emilio Salgari's *Carthage in Flames*), though the buddy relationship between the Roman Fulvio and his muscular slave Maciste distantly evokes that between Mâtho and Spendius. The scenes in which the doors to the mouth of the gigantic statue of Moloch open and close with nightmarish deliberation as each child in turn hurtles into his fiery maw create a satisfying sense of horror. The film is said to have influenced D.W. Griffith in the making of *Intolerance*. In the wider wake of *Salammbô*, a dark question has continued to loom: did the Carthaginians really sacrifice children to Moloch in the horrifying way so dispassionately described by Flaubert? There is something mythical in the idea of a powerful, sophisticated, but threatened culture resorting to these most atrocious of measures. But there is no need to resort to myth. As Flaubert's main source, Polybius, put it, 'In the end, there is no beast more wicked or cruel than man.' It was not only in a distant, faraway, exotic culture that living children have been thrown into the flames.

Salammbô: Battle for Carthage is now a computer game by Dreamcatcher Interactive. It fittingly embodies several aspects of the novel: its mineral exoticism, its hieratic sexiness, its fascination with Piranesi-like architecture, and its obsession with extreme violence.

In August 1866, Flaubert was awarded the Cross of the Legion of Honour. So was Viscount Paul Alexis Ponson du Terrail, the greatest literary success of the Second Empire, a one-man writing factory (10,000 pages per year, on average) who wrote for five magazines simultaneously, and produced sentences such as 'Her hands were as cold as those of a snake.' Ponson du Terrail was a little dismayed to realise that he was being honoured at the same time as a man who had actually been put on trial for immorality.

Once the dust raised by Flaubert's 'operation desert storm' had more or less died down, his attention reverted to horrible French modernity, and his latest project, *Sentimental Education*.

He still made the occasional laconic comment on his Carthaginian extravaganza. On 30th October 1867 he wrote to George Sand that the book could do with some of its grammatical inversions being pruned. It felt laboured. 'Too many *thens, buts,* and *ands*.'

Sentimental Education

In the first version of *Sentimental Education*, we meet a black man on the ship taking Henry and Emilie to New York. His father had sold him for a bag of nails; he had then worked as a servant in France. He was given five years' hard labour for stealing a scarf. He was now returning to America, having failed to find his beloved mistress. 'This man too had undergone his sentimental education', notes the text.

This first version focused increasingly, towards its end, on Jules, who becomes something of an aesthetico-pantheistic hermit. 'He gradually withdrew from the concrete, the limited, the finite, to dwell in the abstract, the eternal, the beautiful. [...] He tried to have, for nature, a loving understanding [*une intelligence aimante*], a new faculty, with which he sought to enjoy the whole world as a complete harmony.' Jules chooses the strategic withdrawal of art to the more buccaneering approach of his friend Henry. Flaubert soon decided that such dualisms might be good enough for his letters, but not for a novel. The second *Sentimental Education* was a vast rewrite – almost beyond recognition – of the first; in this later version, schematic oppositions are seen as a problem rather than a solution. Instead of relying on his own experience and imaginings, Flaubert undertook vast quantities of research: over three hundred folios of plans, sketches and drafts, and over a hundred folios of notes taken from a huge array of sources: utopians and socialists,

Saint-Simon and Fourier, Lacordaire and Lamennais. He interviewed workers from the faubourg Saint-Antoine, a cab driver, and men who had fought at the barricades which he himself had witnessed at close quarters. He visited the Jockey Club, the Café Anglais, and the Creil Pottery works. He observed a three-year-old victim of diphtheria in a hospital. George Sand regaled him with memories of her own prominent part in the politics of the Second Republic, and put him in touch with Armand Barbès, the professional plotter and 'thorn in the flesh of the establishment' (said Marx, approvingly) who had forever been joining or founding secret societies with names like the Society of the Rights of Man, the Society of Avengers, the Society of Families, the Society of the Seasons and then the New Seasons. Barbès wrote from his exile in Belgium in response to a request from Flaubert for information, and Flaubert wrote back to thank him, on 8th October 1867, for his 'friendly, cordial and noble letter. I had long thought of you with respect, and now I love you. The details you have sent me will be included (in an incidental way) in a book I'm writing, set between 1840 and 1852.' (He did indeed: the chameleonic conspirator Sénécal joins the Society of Families and takes part in the abortive Society of the Seasons insurrection of 12th May 1839; but the more attractive Dussardier is also inspired by Barbès, and indignantly recounts the story of the latter's mistreatment in the prison on Mont Saint-Michel.) Flaubert told Sand of his 'high opinion' for this man who had been out in the streets while he himself was merely trying out his sentences.

Three weeks later, Flaubert wrote to Princess Mathilde, promising to come and visit her in Paris; he shared her 'political anxieties'.

As the novel begins, Paris vanishes. Frédéric Moreau, eighteen years old, has hardly had time to look at it before returning to Nogent by boat down the Seine. The novels of Balzac, in which the hero's job is to arrive in Paris *from* the provinces, are rewound before our eyes. At the same moment, Frédéric sees Madame

Arnoux on the same vessel, and falls in love: but again, there will be no traditional 'love story' here, but something much more bitty, incomplete, fervent, timeless.

The ironic surveillance under which the characters in *Madame Bovary* had been kept is still active, but more diffuse and less unremitting. Deslauriers, who has trained as a lawyer, is allowed the occasional Latin tag (*'sicut decet'*) without turning into Homais: but then, Deslauriers is a more unassuming character. The *demi-mondaine* Rosanette (a whore since childhood) thinks Lebanon is in China, but she can hardly be expected to know any better. In any case, a decent education is not much use to Frédéric and his friends; even at their most intense, their lives are half-lives. The things the young men say occasionally resemble the comments in Flaubert's letters, and the comments we might want to make about those letters. This is a novel of velleities, of whims, of missed opportunities, of missed appointments, of encounters that never take place, of unspoken passion. There are parties and balls: none of them have the aura with which Emma Bovary invests that at La Vaubyessard. There are none of the great set pieces of *Madame Bovary*: instead, in various rooms, women come and go (the 1862 plan noted 'a circle of women talking of serious matters'). Homer had catalogued the ships that sailed from Greece for Troy: Flaubert catalogues the vehicles on the Champs-Élysées. The debates (for what they were worth) in *Madame Bovary* tended to be polarised: Homais versus Bournisien, Science versus Religion. Here there are many more options: a babble of student chatter, a plethora of political positions, a charivari of opinions. The number forty-three plays an important but enigmatic role, as it had in *Madame Bovary* (there were forty-three guests at Emma's wedding, and she was ill for forty-three days after her abandonment by Roldolphe): it is probably not even a signifier of insignificance. Although Mme Arnoux plays the piano and sings, the art of *Sentimental Education* is not (as it had been in *Madame Bovary*) music, but painting (and, more generally, the visual arts), thanks to the presence of Pellerin: he produces a considerable number of theories about art, and few concrete artworks – or perhaps he is already anticipating the development of conceptual art.

In Part II, chapter one, Flaubert describes how a newly wealthy Frédéric now feels he is in a position to declare his love to Madame Arnoux. He rushes back to Paris, and spends six pages trying to find where she can be. He consults directories, several friends, various art dealers (M. Arnoux is in the art business); criss-crosses rainy Paris, tries the police station, and hangs around in several cafés – in just one he swallows, in rapid succession, a glass of rum, one of kirsch, one of curaçao, and several kinds of punch both hot and cold, before realising he is in quite the wrong place. Flaubert details this sequence of non-events with remorseless precision: Frédéric's frustrations are comic, and he does eventually track down the object of her desire: seeing her again is a terrible anti-climax. These pages foreshadow large swathes of Proust, Beckett and the tenacious cartographical zest of Perec.

And yet, behind all the talking, the zigzaggings across Paris, the projects and people taken up and laid aside, things do happen. Frédéric takes Rosanette (available) to the boudoir which he had arrayed for Madame Arnoux (inaccessible): as they walk down the rue Caumartin (it is 23rd February 1848 and must be about half past nine in the evening) they hear the noise of gunfire behind them. The text tells us that this was the 'fusillade' on the boulevard des Capucines; we know from other sources that a detachment of soldiers shot and killed between eighty and a hundred people. Historically, it was at this moment that the rioting turned into a revolution. Frédéric says merely, 'Ah! A few bourgeois are getting it in the neck.' (Flaubert had been walking in that area with Maxime and Louis that same night; they too had heard the sound of gunfire, but Max had thought it was children letting off fireworks; – and they had spent the night in Du Camp's apartment, listening as Louis read from his poem *Melaenis*.) The original plan for the novel that Flaubert had drawn up in 1862 noted, 'Show that Sentimentalism (its develop-ment since 1830) follows Politics & reproduces its phases' – the personal as the political. A sentimental education should also be an education in politics (and *Sentimental Education*, together with Dostoyevsky's *The Devils* and the complete works of Kafka, is one of the crucial texts for an understanding of modern politics). When the Republic is declared, Rosanette immediately declares her allegiance to it: 'Monseigneur the Archbishop of Paris had already done so, and, with amazing alacrity, so would the following: the Magistrature, the Council of State, the Insti-tute, the Marshals of France, Changarnier, M. de Falloux, all the Bonapartistes, all the Legitimists, and a considerable number of Orleanists.' Rosanette, the kept woman, joins all the others who know which side their bread is buttered, in a satirical list worthy of Karl Marx.

The novel's first epiphany is one of love (Frédéric's *coup de foudre* at seeing Madame Arnoux – on a Seine riverboat, as Flaubert's fluminal and aquatic penchants might lead us to expect). Its second is one of power. Behind all the student chat-ter, the world changes. Frédéric, having abandoned Paris for an idyll with Rosanette in the Forest of Fontainebleau (they wander through the ancient trees, pondering the vast stretches of geo-logical time: the historical upheavals of Paris seem very distant), hears that Deslauriers has been wounded and rushes back just in time to witness the fusillades on the boulevard. Dragoons are sweeping down the boulevards as the crowd looks on, 'mute, terrified'. One man, on the steps of Tortoni's, refuses to accept the imposition of the new status quo, cries 'Vive la République!', and is cut down by a man in uniform. He falls with his arms '*en croix*' – a real crux for the translator, since 'flung out as on a cross' may be a little excessive, or not. Frédéric recognises both of them, the killer and his victim, as friends of his. The first is the idealistic leftwinger Dussardier ('the revolutionist Dussardier is depicted in a positive light', as the *Great Soviet Encyclopaedia* put it); the second is Sénécal, who has been throughout the novel slowly shifting political position from extreme left to a supporter of the new regime. This revelation – of pure political force, of the tragedy of idealism and the triumph of *Realpolitik* – leaves Frédéric *'béant'*, aghast, open-mouthed. 'He travelled', says the text, after an ellipsis of considerable power: so did many others after the *coup d'état*, not all of them under their own volition, since some 8,000 were exiled to Algeria or Cayenne.

In May 1848, the Duke of Wellington had said: 'France needs a Napoleon! I cannot yet see him... Where is he?' Here he was, Louis Napoleon, the adventurer seizing his chance, the invisible finally made manifest in a cavalry charge along the boulevards, as yet another French regime was inaugurated in bloodshed – not for the last time.

The novel did not garner good reviews. Flaubert was taken aback, 'surprised at all the hatred and dishonesty' shown by the critics. But just as he had turned against *Madame Bovary*, his opinion of *Sentimental Education* dipped: trying to explain the low sales figures for the novel, he claimed, a year before his death, that it was 'too true'; and, 'aesthetically speaking, *it lacks the falseness of perspective*'. It had no peaks, it was not 'a pyramid'. It is true that the architectonics of *Madame Bovary* are replaced by a haze of fleeting details, but these can then be integrated into vast and varied structures. As with serialism in music, the apparent dissonances, aimless structure and lack of resolution force the reader to look elsewhere, to structures other than tonality (or narrative).

It is the novel for shnorrers and schmucks, kvetchers and kibitzers. It comes as no surprise to learn that it is one of the things that make life worth living for Isaac in Woody Allen's *Manhattan*. It is also now officially part of Revelation: Kafka, who found that the life in the novel seeped into him, compared its final pages to Moses on Mount Pisgah, gazing at a Palestine that he would never enter.

Flaubert's state of mind in his last years can partly be gauged from a diary note he made in 1870. 'The idea of suicide is the most consoling of all,' he wrote, before detailing three defections (perhaps of Alfred, Louis and Max). 'The first left me for a woman, the second for a woman, the third for a woman! All of them! Am I a monster then?' Napoleon III was defeated at Sedan; Flaubert turned back to *Saint Anthony*, that drama of saints and monsters. (He stopped wearing his Legion of Honour ribbon for a while, as he felt that France had lost hers.) But he also emerged from melancholy broodings to take part in the defence of his native land from the Prussian invasion. On 17th August he enrolled as a nurse in the Hôtel-Dieu; he even helped to organise a battalion of the *Garde Nationale* and was appointed lieutenant; he drilled his men with zest, and dreamed of rushing to fight under the walls of Paris with them if it was besieged, as it was, by 'the compatriots of Hegel'. (It is not clear how many of the Prussians had read *The Phenomenology of Spirit* or whether, as they lobbed cannon shells at Montmartre, they slapped each other on the back quoting, 'The real is the rational and the rational the real.') By September, the news was that the capital was not going to surrender and the Prussians would concentrate on occupying the provinces, including Rouen. He was impressed by the defiant letters written by soldiers: 'you can't gobble up a country where they write things like that. France is an old nag with vigour that will soon reveal itself.' One minute he was quoting these patriotic slogans, the next turning on them with fierce contempt. He was as *engagé* as the men under his command, but continued to be an *enragé*, furious with everyone and everything. His letters to Caroline and to George Sand reveal a man thrown into disarray, too old to adapt to the 'new world' he sensed was about to emerge: it would, he noted presciently, be utilitarian, military, American and Catholic (the last epithet was correct at least in France, which indulged in an orgy of penitent religiosity after the defeat of the Commune). Latin civilisation would lose out to Prussian discipline, science and positivism.

In September 1870 he lay reading Walter Scott, as the Prussians advanced towards Rouen. He became obsessed by the idea that he was ill with cancer, or losing his mind. They arrived on 5th December; ten soldiers were billeted on Croisset five days later. He was overcome by fits of weeping, and suffered the indignity of having to fetch hay and straw for their horses. On 29th January 1871, Paris finally surrendered after a protracted and agonising siege in which the population had slowly starved: no more Carthaginian feasts – or rather, the 'vermin eaters' of *Salammbô* were now a common sight in the streets of the capital, and restaurants served consommé of horse, brochettes of dogs' liver, *salmis* of rats, and even bear. (Edmond de Goncourt consumed an elephant sausage for dinner: the elephants in the zoo had been slaughtered for food.) The Germans marched down the Champs-Élysées on 1st March 1871. Flaubert claimed he would have preferred the whole city to have been burned down rather than suffer such dishonour; he wished he could disappear, and contemplated, as second best, writing to Turgenev and finding out whether he could become a Russian citizen. He left Croisset for Rouen and hoped that the Prussians did not wreck his beloved house (they drank his champagne, swiped some of his pipes, and scattered his books about, but nothing worse: his notes on *Saint Anthony* and the trunk full of letters that he had buried remained intact). The Commune was proclaimed and Paris was immediately invested by the Versailles Government, provoking a civil war; Flaubert saw the Commune as a recrudescence of the Middle Ages, not just because the word 'commune' referred to a medieval political entity but because it now represented a mystical-apocalyptic, visionary and destructive movement. The Communards' reforms included women's right to vote, the abolition of night work in bakeries, education and technical training to be made free for all. He hated their socialism, he hated democracy (the rule of mere number): the best France could hope for was 'a legitimate aristocracy'. The Second Empire had deserved to perish: everything was fake – 'fake realism, fake army, fake credit, even fake whores'. But the new disorder was worse than the old, false order. 'Always gods! Always slogans!' He wished he could drown the Communards in the latrines. And yet they were merely trying to abolish life as a *pensum* – and their absolutism and violence were, as he occasionally sensed, akin to his own. The eleventh edition of the *Encyclopaedia Britannica* refers to the Communards as a set of disparate groups united in 'their vague but perpetual hostility to the existing order of things'. They were clearly *bovarystes*, or even Flaubertians. As, during the *Semaine Sanglante*, they retreated to their last strongholds in Belleville and Ménilmontant and finally the cemetery of Père Lachaise, the Versailles troops exacted their vengeance: 43,000 prisoners were taken, about 30,000 were killed, and, in the summary trials following the uprising, nearly 4,000 deported to New Caledonia. Sartre would later hold Flaubert and the Goncourts responsible because they did not write a single line of protest against the repression. Flaubert might have replied that he had already protested, in the scenes of imprisonment and violence in *Sentimental Education* – but perhaps that is special pleading. (According to Du Camp, as the two men surveyed the blackened ruins of the Tuileries, Flaubert said that none of this would have happened if people had only understood *Sentimental Education*: this is no doubt true, but it is not clear what people would ever actually do if they really understood Flaubert's great novel.)

Saint Anthony, that panorama of ideas for which people had lived and died through the ages, sustained him with thoughts of higher, or at least different, things. On 6th June 1871, a week after the final crushing of the Commune, Flaubert wrote to Renan, asking for information about Buddhism to include in his survey of world religions.

Saint Anthony

Saint Anthony had accompanied Flaubert since childhood; it had sustained him through the events of 1848 and the catastrophe of 1870–1; by the time he finished it, his mother ('the person I loved most') was dead. It is his secret history: it is perhaps, also, a secret history of the world. Although he identified with his saint, Flaubert was, as a writer, a monk reversed: it was the secular that caused him difficulty, whereas, being a simple soul, his natural milieu was the fantastic and the supernatural. Anthony lives in a world where sacred and profane are indistinguishable (or, to put it another way, there is only the sacred). He dreams of travel, of life, of other lives, of others' lives: but they remain mere representations. When he seems to succumb, as to a vision of vast wealth, the gold and jewels simply evaporate. Like Nietzsche, Flaubert raises the question 'what do ascetic ideas mean?' and like Freud and Weber he muses on the way the human beings of modernity are essentially ascetics who have merely internalised their gods and devils (and maybe made them even more ineradicable than before). The Queen of Sheba tells Anthony she 'dances like a bee' – but she also tempts him with visions that repeat those of Emma and Rodolphe (the Queen has 'a pavilion on a promontory in the middle of an isthmus, between two oceans' and beckons him to share it with her: 'we would sleep on duvets softer than the clouds, we would drink cold drinks from the rinds of fruits, and we would gaze at the sun through emeralds!' – a Sunday colour supplement world). The saint is no Faust: he is distinctly underwhelmed ('What's it to me?' 'So...?') by Simon Magus' tale of Helen of Troy. His orthodoxy blinds him to possibilities of other lives, or saves him from other illusions: Apollonius of Tyana tempts him to see Jesus as Being itself, but Anthony clings to the cross. We are tempted to become students of comparative religion and conclude that all of these gods and goddesses and hobgoblins belong to a waning world: all are equally illusory, Jesus as much as Buddha – but the person who draws this parallel is Hilarion, and there is a whiff of the diabolical about him... In Flaubert's earliest works, it was always the Devil who offered the most encyclopaedic visions, the most panoptic surveys, the world and all its glories as seen from a great height (from a temple, or a mountain peak, or maybe a pyramid): what if sceptical liberal relativism (irony, the aesthetic) were, not a safe haven from which to laugh at the ship of fools, but itself *devilish*? And yet the text is not simply a semi-dramatised dictionary of mythology: even though its denizens often run on stage, shout their slogans and then vanish, Anthony thinks about what he sees: there is a subtle process of imagistic reflection at work, and a real affection for some of the deities of vanished worlds. Nerval, in his 'mad' text 'Aurélia', had asked God to preserve the pagan gods, Baldur, son of Odin, and Freya the beautiful: Flaubert registers the beauty and pathos of Isis, and the death of Harpocrates, the god of silence, is invested with tragic intensity.

At the end, Anthony is tempted by the Devil in person, whose jaws are open to devour him. Anthony gazes upwards in 'a last movement of hope' – and the Devil disappears. Whereupon, the saint is granted an epiphany which seems to explode with the happiness of nature at its most endlessly proliferating, inventive, and monstrous: bubbles called Astomi, half-creatures known as Nisnas and headless Blemmyes (who are still quite capable of speech); there are pygmies and sciapods – and the Catoblepas, a vast, flabby, inert blob whose stupidity the Saint finds alluring.

In a startling anticipation of modern physics, Anthony sees the string-like vibrations of which the world is comprised; he sees life being born, and longs to be united with it; he wants to *be* matter, no longer to see it as representation – and then he sees Christ, a distant figure in the sky. Perhaps Christ is the Last Temptation of Anthony, or the only escape from temptation: either way, he is still a representation, and the text cannot depict the fusion for which Anthony (who docilely falls back to his prayers) yearns. And yet this *Twilight of the Idols*, which in Flaubert's view (if we are to believe Edmond de Goncourt) ended with yet another 'defeat' – the saint is *'délirant'*, delirious or crazy, during his final epiphany – also concludes with a subdued and enigmatic sense of benediction. Méliès made a film of it, in 1898.

Flaubert's last decade was the decade of saints. He wrote so much about them that he was becoming, he wrote, a new 'Church Father'. There was, most spectacularly, Saint Anthony; there were also Saints Julian and John the Baptist, not to mention the (possibly) saintly Félicité, of the *Three Tales*. But the patron saint that he chose for himself was Saint Polycarp, a Bishop of Smyrna martyred in AD 167 and a doughty opponent of the Gnostics – though this was not why Flaubert identified with him. Rather, he had come across an old engraving for sale on the quaysides of the Seine, in which the saint was exclaiming, perhaps apocryphally: 'My God! My God! My God! In what an age you have made me live!'

Ruin

In 1875, Flaubert and his brother Achille discovered that Ernest Commanville, husband of their niece Caroline, had built up debts of some one and a half million francs. Like many others in the speculative, profiteering Second Empire, he had played the system and lost. Flaubert, devoted to his niece, did what he could to cushion her financial fall, giving up his inheritance on her behalf. Money problems cast their shadows over the last years of his life. He enlightened the gloom with a dark satire.

Bouvard and Pécuchet

Two copyists unexpectedly find themselves rich, thanks to an inheritance. They retire to the countryside and try to farm the land on their new property. The mistakes they make lead them to try to understand the science of agriculture; but, like Jules in the first *Sentimental Education*, though in a more baneful sense, they realise that everything is interlinked: in order to understand agriculture, they need to study landscape gardening and food preservation, then chemistry, then anatomy, medicine, biology, geology and astronomy, archaeology, architecture, history (they plan a biography of the Duc d'Angoulême), and literature (drama, grammar, and general aesthetics). The February Revolution of 1848 impels them to study politics; they fall in love; they indulge in gymnastics, study health and diet, hypnotism, occultism and sorcery, theology and philosophy. A crisis of scepticism leads them to the verge of suicide and then religion; their faith soon wanes, and they turn to education, trying to bring up two orphans, Victor and Victorine. (Some scholars have worked out that Bouvard and Pécuchet must be about eighty by this stage.) This last endeavour also meets with defeat; they struggle to continue their studies (music, town planning), but by now have alienated everyone in their village (they are even threatened by prison), and exhausted the circle of the sciences. With joy and relief they turn back to their initial profession of copying – but now they will copy simply for themselves, sitting together at a desk made for two. It is said that the words 'Let's copy as before' were added to the text by Flaubert's niece after his death.

Flaubert told a correspondent that the novel could be subtitled 'On the Lack of Method in the Sciences'; but he needed the usual piles of documentation to ascertain what the 'sciences' said so that he could deride it, or show his two 'woodlice' heroes misunderstanding it, or merely present it. One of the more neutral aspects of the book, and of the *sottisier* that, in different guises, Flaubert compiled throughout his life, was the way it enabled him to present many different kinds of discourse – aesthetic, scientific, legal, political, medical: he was the son and brother of specialists, but he was a novelist whose only specialism was words. This everlasting amateur can hardly be taken as a secure guide to the forms of knowledge he deploys: his research was both furious and superficial. Can anyone really understand agriculture just by trying out a few prescriptions from a textbook and then, when these don't work, giving up? Most of human history has not given people any chance to give up and move onto something else, the opportunity of which Bouvard and Pécuchet avail themselves every chapter or so. But by juxtaposing these different languages, Flaubert illuminates the world in which, in all their uncommunicative and yet oddly interlinked way, they coexist.

Flaubert intended the book to be a counterpart to *Saint Anthony*. In that work he had paraded, one after another, ancient religions and philosophies; he here does the same for the ideas of modernity. It is 'the Tower of Babel' of science, said Maupassant. It is also a grandiose rewrite of *Candide* (which Flaubert claimed to have translated into English as a young man): Bouvard and Pécuchet, like the innocent hero of Voltaire's novel, are intrigued by ideas (just as Candide is all too eager to accept Pangloss's teaching about this being 'the best of all possible worlds'), but constantly find that the least little experience contradicts those ideas. At least, that is what they think they find: in fact, they are impatient, and conclude too quickly.

Maupassant's other comments on Flaubert's last work are also good guides. 'Whoever has written on any subject whatever has sometimes said something stupid [*une sottise*]. Flaubert had infallibly found it out.' This is Flaubert the arch-corrector, the manic schoolteacher wielding a red pen on even the most hallowed works of literature (including, when he found a flower blooming in the wrong season in *Madame Bovary*, himself). Everything becomes guilty by association: culture is *nothing but* a series of mistakes and misapprehensions. When Bouvard and Pécuchet return to their jobs as copyists, it is this *sottisier* that they compile. Copying in a scriptorium: we are back in the Middle Ages, in the shadow of the spire. Maupassant encapsulates Flaubert's method in a few evocative words: it was essentially a matter of distilling, by alchemy, vast, cumbersome tracts into fifty lapidary sentences. He 'melted down and mixed together', he 'rejected the inessential ideas and simplified the main ones'. But surely the classics in paraphrase are bound to seem, in turn, clumsy, cursory and comic? By using free indirect style on the ideas that beguile his two heroes, Flaubert reminds us that ideas are only as good as the minds that receive them. Bouvard and Pécuchet are no less inept than Emma or Frédéric: it is just that their subject-matter is more varied, and their margins for error consequently so much broader.

Flaubert shared the mania for knowledge (for book-learning), and the awareness of its limits, with his heroes. Like Bouvard and Pécuchet, he watched as the words that had inspired so many dreams emptied themselves of content. By the time the Third Republic had been established on the ruin of the Second Empire, political cataclysms had shown up the futility of ideological postures. 'The words religion or Catholicism, on the one hand, progress, fraternity, democracy, on the other, no longer correspond to the spiritual demands of the present time... I can see no means of establishing a new principle today, nor of respecting the old principles.' And yet he persisted in his quest. 'So I seek, without finding it, the idea on which everything else must hang.'

This quest produced one of the greatest comic novels ever written. *Bouvard and Pécuchet*, rather than *Madame Bovary*, is Flaubert's *Don Quixote* (in which it is a bumbling pair of Sancho Panzas who have assumed the role of the quixotic don). Its bright, hectic fierceness is imbued with a weird serenity; but the wrath and contempt which had always driven Flaubert to create are terrifying to read. 'We need to send mankind to hell, since it does the same to us. Oh! I'll get my revenge! I'll get my revenge!' he had written to Louise Colet in 1853, promising a 'big modern novel' that would be the vehicle of that vengeance. Two years later, to Louis Bouilhet: 'I sense floods of hatred for the stupidity of my period, and I'm drowning in them. Shit keeps rising to my mouth, as in strangulated hernias. But I want to keep that shit, fix it, harden it; I want to make it into a paste with which I'd smear the 19th century, in the same way that they decorate Indian pagodas with cow-dung.' And he was writing *Bouvard and Pécuchet* – he told another correspondent in October 1872 – 'with the sole aim of spitting out at my contemporaries the disgust with which they fill me. I'm finally going to tell them the way I think, exhale my resentment, vomit out my hatred, expectorate my bile, ejaculate my anger, cleanse out my indignation. I'm not a man, I am dynamite!' No, he did not actually write the last sentence: that was Nietzsche, in *Ecce Homo*: but there is the same orgasm of anger, the same eruption of a disdained prophet's fury, the same euphoric, crazed assault on an entire culture. But Flaubert was more methodical: *Bouvard and Pécuchet* was a 'kind of encyclopaedia of modern stupidity', he wrote: 'you can see that the subject is limitless'.

Turgenev protested that the novel would be more effective if it were shorter; but Flaubert did not want to write a 'witty' piece, 'concise and light'; he wanted to give the impression of believing in his story, which needed to be serious, detailed, perhaps even 'scary'.

The novel's genesis was as painful as usual. Within nine months of starting writing, he had dragged himself through stomach aches and a growing sense of desolation to the end of the first chapter. He told Edma Roger des Genettes that his two copyists had taken him over: he was them, their stupidity was his, and it was killing him. He was struggling to provide the book with some kind of narrative continuity – otherwise it would seem like a 'philosophical dissertation'. 'What drives me to despair is that I no longer believe in my book. The sight of all the difficulties that lie ahead is crushing me in advance.' And the old word returns: 'it's become a *pensum* for me.'

What exactly do the copyists at the end copy? (It is as if Don Quixote were to return to La Mancha and spend the rest of his life copying out old tales of chivalry, on the principle of 'the hair of the dog that bit you'). Maupassant had access to Flaubert's notes, and says that they were already classified (into categories such as 'Ethics', 'Love', 'Philosophy', 'Socialism (religious and political)', etc.) and included 'specimens of style' ('paraphrases', 'palinodes', 'rococo'), and examples of different styles ('classical', 'scientific', 'medical', 'clerical', 'revolutionary', 'official style of sovereigns', etc.), together with a 'History of Scientific Ideas', a section on the 'Fine Arts', 'opinions on great men'; 'bizarre ideas', 'ferocities', 'eccentricities', 'insults', and a major section called 'IMBECILES', including the 'Dictionary of received ideas' and 'The catalogue of fashionable [*chic*] ideas'.

Flaubert had noted down quotations from a wide range of authors: Proudhon claims that 'the women in Egypt prostituted themselves in public to crocodiles'; De Maistre, in 1807, argues that Prussia was a spent force; Condillac wrote of Corneille that 'in spite of the reputation enjoyed by this writer, there is a great deal of negligence in his style'. He picked up a quotation from Scribe who, on being received into the French Academy, wondered why Molière's plays had nothing to teach us about the Revocation of the Edict of Nantes. Flaubert wrote under this quotation: 'Revocation of the Edict of Nantes, 1685. Death of Molière, 1671'. Do these statements belong in a *sottisier*? They all have their rationale (Prussia probably *did* seem a spent force in 1807), or else are, like Scribe's, a matter of mistaken fact (of scribal error). Perhaps what Flaubert detested was their directness, their assertiveness: they pass themselves off as uncontroversial and clear, or else they simply offer matters of opinion with a dogmatic flourish. Flaubert refuses to allow his authors to argue their case. Such statements may seem banal, but they can be oppressive. Their anonymity is not the indirection of the aesthetic, but a pervasive generalness. 'In the course of the whole book, there mustn't be a single word of my own invention, and once people have read it they won't dare speak again, for fear of uttering quite naturally one of the phrases in it.' Flaubert, who had tried to make the stones of Carthage speak, here imposes silence on his contemporaries – or rather shows how, when at any moment an infinite number of speech acts is possible, they silence themselves by resorting to platitudes. The idea of the preface he would write to this Dictionary (which itself he sometimes envisaged as a prolegomenon, or appendix, or stand-in for a novel on a broad canvas in which he would yield to his 'atrocious itch to bellow at [engueuler] human beings') gave him considerable excitement; it would be an entire book in itself. He would attack everything (but, even though he might be run out of Europe, no law could attack him in turn). It would be 'the historical glorification of everything that meets with approval'. He would show that majorities are always right and minorities wrong; that mediocrity in literature is accessible to all and thus preferable to originality. The work would be 'full of quotations, of proofs (that would prove the opposite) and terrifying texts (this would be easy)'. In it, you would find, on every conceivable subject, 'everything that you need to say in society to be a respectable and likeable man'. Examples: ARTISTS: are all disinterested. FRANCE: needs an iron fist to be governed. ERECTION: said only when talking of monuments.

Three Tales

The three stories that Flaubert wrote as a break from *Bouvard and Pécuchet* were the work that brought him the most uncomplicated acclaim. It is sometimes claimed that he wrote them relatively quickly. Relatively, maybe: the thirty pages of 'A Simple Heart' cost 900 hours of work. His research was as thorough as ever. For 'Herodias', the story about the martyrdom of John the Baptist, he consulted a library of learned tomes, including *The history of Our Lord as exemplified in works of art: with that of His types; St. John the Baptist; and other persons of the Old and New Testament*, commenced by the late Mrs Jameson, continued and completed by Lady Eastlake (2 vols, 1864). Mrs Jameson also wrote *The Diary of an Ennuyée* (1826). He also delved into Blasio Ugolini's *Thesaurus antiquitam sacrarum complectens selectissima… opuscula in quibus veterum Hebraerorum mores, leges, instituta, ritus sacri et civiles illustrantur*, J.-G. Hertz et S. Coletti, 1744–1769, in thirty-three volumes. It was as if 'Herodias' was to be a fifth gospel, and every bit as precise and historically accurate as the four canonical ones.

All three stories end with epiphanies. Félicité's stuffed parrot, the signifier of all the people she has loved in her life, hovers over her as she dies, like the Holy Spirit. This is often seen as idolatry and fetishism (Huizinga remarked, in *The Waning of the Middle Ages*: 'This familiarity with sacred things is, on the one hand, a sign of deep and ingenuous faith; on the other, it entails irreverence whenever mental contact with the infinite fails'). On the other hand, a religion of incarnation can cope with a little irony, and is more tolerant of apparent kitsch than is the religion of art: Aquinas points out that there can never be enough images of an unimaginable God (the problems – the risk of idolatry – occur only when one of these images is taken literally). In any case, the parrot is indeed an ancient and hallowed symbol in Christian art, visible in the *Madonna of Canon van Paele* by Van Eyck, in Martin Schongauer's *Madonna with the Parrot* (c. 1474), in Hans Baldung's *Madonna with a Parrot*, and in the *Virgin and Child* of 1520 by the aptly-named Master of the Parrot. It was also, in Flaubert's own day, an erotic creature, bringing Félicité the fulfilment she has so signally lacked: Courbet's *La Femme au Perroquet* was shown in the Salon of 1866, and the artist was criticised for his lack of taste; his model's pose (she lies on her back, her pert breasts pointing up at the parrot nibbling the fingers of her upheld left hand) was ungainly, and her hair dishevelled. Cézanne carried a photograph of it in his wallet, and Manet produced his own version in *Young Lady in 1866 (Woman with a Parrot)*. God is sometimes treated as the parrot of human desires, but not always in a bad sense, and Félicité's Loulou is a welcome addition to that noble company, the Dead Parrots' Society.

'Saint Julian' ends, as we have seen, with a leper turning into Christ; and 'Herodias' is a story about what can and cannot be represented – like the other two stories it is an investigation into the Second Commandment (here the Jews object violently to the Roman standards in the Temple). At the end, John the Baptist's head is carried off to Jesus in Galilee, amid a flurry of quotations from the scriptures and presentments of a new dispensation that put a new and urgent spin on the world of fact. Despite all his research, Flaubert overrides his sources just as some of the followers of John and Jesus wrenched the prophecies into strange and enticing new meanings. In this way, under the immense pressure exerted from other dimensions, a religion comes into being. This is how art is born, too. Someone had suggested to Flaubert that the equation between parrot and Holy Spirit was if anything 'too subtle' for an old peasant woman: Flaubert agreed, and stayed up all night blackening twenty pages in an attempt to find a new way of putting it. But he gave up: it would be necessary to change the 'harmony' of his sentences, and, as he also insisted, 'Too bad for the meaning: rhythm comes first!' The pressure of another dimension (symbolic or musical) is just as real as the *données* of the narrative.

Flaubert's realism continued to be visionary, even hallucinatory (he read several works on hallucination while writing the *Three Tales*). On 17th August 1876 he wrote 'and *I can see* (clearly, as I see the Seine) the surface of the Dead Sea glittering in the sun. Herod and his wife are on a balcony, from which the gilded tiles of the Temple can be seen.'

In 1877 he told the Goncourts he was planning a novel about the Second Empire, using Lesur's *Annuaire* and *La Vie Parisienne* by Marcelin. In 1879 he was dreaming of writing a Battle of Thermopylae. He told Edmond de Goncourt that he would go back to Greece to do fieldwork (he had already visited the site): 'I want to write it without resorting to technical terms, without using, for instance, the word *cnemides*. In those Greek warriors I see a doomed band, going to their deaths in a gay, ironic way... This book must be for all peoples a MARSEILLAISE of an elevated kind!' He planned an 'Anubis', and fictions with titles such as 'The Three Grocers', 'Microscopic Animals', 'A Racist Drama in the U.S.A.' (he hated *Uncle Tom's Cabin*), 'Parisian Life and Customs', '*La Blague*' ('The Hoax', or 'The Practical Joke'). But art is long and life is brief.

On 15th February 1880, Flaubert wrote to Caroline: 'For a fortnight now I've been gripped by the yearning to see a palm tree standing out against a blue sky and to hear a stork's beak clacking on the summit of a minaret... How much good it would do me, physically and mentally!'

On Easter Sunday (28th March) 1880, Daudet, Zola, Charpentier and Edmond de Goncourt went out to Croisset.

Flaubert met them with 'a big affectionate expression on his face'. They ate a marvellous *sauce à la crème d'un turbot*, seasoned with spicy anecdotes. When Flaubert saw them off, he gave Goncourt a bear-hug; Goncourt saw, or fancied he saw, a tear in his eye. He again noted Flaubert's childlike laughter.

On 8th May he received a telegram: FLAUBERT MORT.

Influence

Flaubert influenced everybody.

He was one of the most important figures in European literature as the *fin de siècle* (when the two strands which his work had held in tension, realism and surrealism, started to diverge) mutated into High Modernism (when they were yoked again together, forcibly). Joseph Conrad memorised whole pages of *Madame Bovary*. While writing *The Nigger of the Narcissus*, he read *Salammbô* every day as if it were 'my morning office'. We have seen how Kafka saw him as a kind of father figure (for once, Flaubert would not have roared with dismay at bringing progeny into the world). Proust, though sniffy about Flaubert's rather coarse ironies, saw his love of the imperfect (in every sense) as a revolution; Flaubert's use of grammar was a discovery on a par with Kant's Copernican shift in philosophy, and in itself renovated our sense of reality. Flaubert was the 'true Penelope' of Pound's Hugh Selwyn Mauberley: style is a matter of fishing 'by obstinate isles'. Joyce, the eternal *Besserwisser* (rather like Flaubert) once met the French writer Edmond Jaloux who had a copy of the *Trois Contes* in his pocket. Over a glass or three of white wine, Jaloux started singing the praises of Flaubert's style. 'He's not *that* good,' protested Joyce, and proceeded to claim (incorrectly) that both the first sentence of 'A Simple Heart' and the last sentence of 'Herodias' were grammatically incorrect. Perhaps Joyce was a little *jaloux*? And yet *Ulysses* is an attempt to release the demons, monsters and angels of *Saint Anthony* into the backstreets of Dublin: it begins with Stephen pondering the heresies that had beset the *unam sanctam*; Bloom owes something to Charles, and Bouvard and Pécuchet, and even Homais; and Molly is a Dublin Emma. Above all, the word 'yes' is no longer just a word uttered by a pretentious pharmacist in a language he only pretends to understand. (In *Finnegans Wake*, of course, the search for the *mot juste* becomes the quest for the *mot joyced*.) George Perec's novels are haunted by Flaubert, and, like all of Flaubert's followers, he also discreetly teases the master: his novel *Life: A User's Manual* includes a 'sentimental painter' called G.F. Pellerin, who has the same dates (1821–80) as Flaubert.

Some characters in Nabokov smoke 'Salammbô': a fashionable brand of cigarettes.

And today? Dreams and desires, sex and shopping, titanic wars fought in faraway deserts as a diamond-encrusted skull grins at us from an unmade bed: this is Flaubert territory. The Middle Ages refuse to wane, the world is still not disenchanted. Flaubert also has his own brand-new bridge, the Pont Gustave Flaubert, over the river Seine at Rouen: a marvel of precision engineering, worthy of the great *flèche* on the cathedral.

Flaubert left behind him thousands of pages of manuscript, and the Buddha who had presided over his study, long ears dangling, eyes half closed, legs crossed, his right hand touching the earth, in the *mudra* which means *I have conquered Mara*. Mara is the embodiment of unskilful emotions, of birth-and-death, and of temptation.

A few years later, a monument to him was inaugurated at the Hôtel-Dieu. Edmond de Goncourt travelled there by train with Zola, Maupassant, Daudet and others. He noted that Maupassant was not looking well; he also noted that the occasion, with its tent, its authorities, and its fairground music, was a bit like the agricultural show in *Madame Bovary*. In his speech, he said: 'In the novel, Flaubert was not merely a painter of contemporary life, he was, like Carlyle and Michelet, a resurrectionist of old worlds, of vanished civilisations, of dead societies [*humanités*]. He enabled us to relive Carthage and the daughter of Hamilcar, the Thebaid and its hermit, the Europe of the Middle Ages and its Julian Hospitator.' He had supported 'us writers against the attacks of critics who had often subjected him to a 'moral cruci-fixion' (a journalist who claimed that Flaubert's prose dishon-oured the reign of Napoleon III, a review that rebuked him for his 'epileptic style'). Flaubert was 'basically kind' and, sacrificing his fortune and his well-being to his family, could be said to have practised 'all the bourgeois virtues' – though the word might offend his shade. Gentlemen, continued Goncourt, M. Chapu, the sculptor, has dedicated all his skill and talent to this sculpture of the novelist's powerful head 'and the elegant allegory of Truth preparing to inscribe the name Gustave Flaubert in the book of Immortality'.

Goncourt's dedication was followed by a tactful address by the mayor of Rouen and then another speech, some twenty-five times as long as Goncourt's, by a representative of the Academy of Rouen, containing 'every cliché, every commonplace, every worn-out expression, every *Homaiserie* imaginable'. On the Day of Resurrection, Flaubert will give him a sound thrashing, and all the rest of us too – no, Goncourt did not write the last bit; but he did tell his journal that, frankly, Chapu's monument was a 'pretty little bas-relief in sugar, on which Truth looks as if she's crapping into a well'. *The New York Times* (8th December 1890) covered the 'simple and touching' inauguration of the Flaubert memorial. It quoted a comment by Maupassant: '*il faut lire ces hommes et ne pas bavarder sur eux*' – 'one should read men like Flaubert rather than chatter about them'.

Marcel Duchamp, from Haute-Normandie, is buried in the same cemetery in Rouen. Ah, these Normans! They're all such rogues!

Bibliography

I have drawn heavily on previous biographies of Flaubert, especially three excellent works:

Brombert, Victor H., *Flaubert par lui-même* (Paris: Éditions du Seuil, 1971)
Brown, Frederick, *Flaubert: a biography* (London: Pimlico, 2007)
Wall, Geoffrey, *Flaubert. A Life* (London: Faber, 2001).

Sartre's great, not to say *'énorme'* biography of Flaubert, is available in English translation:

Sartre, Jean-Paul, *The Family Idiot: Gustave Flaubert, 1821–1857*, 5 vols, translated by Carol Cosman (Chicago and London: University of Chicago Press, 1981–1993)

as is the remarkable attempt to situate Flaubert and his work in the 'field' of mid-19th-century France:

Bourdieu, Pierre, *The Rules of Art: genesis and structure of the literary field*, translated by Susan Emanuel (Cambridge: Polity Press, 1996).

I have also drawn on the entertaining memoirs produced by Flaubert's contemporaries, especially:

Du Camp, Maxime, *Souvenirs littéraires*, edited by Daniel Oster (Paris: Aubier, 1994)
Goncourt, Edmond de, and Jules de, *Journal: mémoires de la vie littéraire*, 3 vols, edited by Robert Ricatte (Paris: Laffont, 1989).

But my main source has been Flaubert's correspondence, as published in the Conard and Pléiade editions:

Flaubert, Gustave, *Correspondance*, edited by Caroline Franklin-Grout, 9 vols (Paris: L. Conard, 1926–33)
Flaubert, Gustave, *Correspondance*, edited by Jean Bruneau and Yvan Leclerc, 5 vols (Paris: Gallimard, 'Pléiade', 1973–2007)

and in various translated selections from the letters:

Flaubert, Gustave, *Selected Letters*, edited and translated by Geoffrey Wall (London: Penguin, 1997)

Flaubert, Gustave, and Ivan Sergeyevich Turgenev, *Flaubert and Turgenev: a friendship in letters: the complete correspondence*, edited and translated by Barbara Beaumont (London: Athlone, 1985)

Flaubert, Gustave, and George Sand, *Flaubert-Sand: the correspondence of Gustave Flaubert and George Sand*, translated by Francis Steegmuller and Barbara Bray (London: Harvill, 1999)

Steegmuller, Francis, *Flaubert in Egypt: a sensibility on tour: a narrative drawn from Flaubert's travel notes and letters* (London: Penguin, 1996)

as well as various collections of Flaubert's juvenilia and later miscellaneous writings, such as:

Flaubert, Gustave, *Cahier intime de jeunesse: souvenirs, notes et pensées intimes*, edited by G.P. Germain (Paris: Nizet, 1987)

Flaubert, Gustave, *Voyage en Égypte*, edited by Pierre-Marc de Biasi (Paris: B. Grasset, 1991)

Flaubert, Gustave, *Vie et travaux du R.P. Cruchard et autres inédits*, edited by Matthieu Desportes and Yvan Leclerc (Mont-Saint-Aignan: Publications des Universités de Rouen et du Havre, 2005).

Flaubert's working notes can be surveyed in:

Flaubert, Gustave, *Carnets de travail*, edited by Pierre-Marc de Biasi (Paris: Balland, 1988).

I have also used the compendious website dedicated to Flaubert and run by the University of Rouen under the general management of Yvan Leclerc: http://flaubert.univ-rouen.fr/ and including several versions of Flaubert's fictional works, as well as the correspondence. There is also a rich Flaubert website at http://pagesperso-orange.fr/jb.guinot/pages/accueil.html

The translations of Flaubert's fiction into English are all exceptional (but unfortunately too numerous to mention here).

On some of Flaubert's contemporaries, see:

De Senneville, Gérard, *Maxime Du Camp: un spectateur engagé du XIXe siècle* (Paris: Stock, 1996)

Gray, Francine du Plessix, *Rage and Fire: a life of Louise Colet: pioneer feminist, literary star, Flaubert's muse* (London: Hamish Hamilton, 1994)

Jack, Belinda, *George Sand: a woman's life writ large* (London: Vintage, 1999).

Acknowledgments

I would never have finished this little book without the encouragement of Alice Albinia. Golnar Malek, Feng Jiang Dolby, Jaehyuk Lee, and Takashi Watanabe all provided useful information, and Corinne François-Denève supplied me with her usual generous mixture of books and humour. I am also indebted to the 1989 MPhil thesis (University of Hong Kong), 'The literary reception of Flaubert's *Madame Bovary* in China', by May-Tak Kwan. None of these people are in any way responsible for my own *bêtise*.

Biographical note

Andrew Brown works as a teacher and a translator. His translations for Hesperus include Gustave Flaubert's *November*, Stendhal's *Letters to Pauline*, André Gide's *Theseus*, Prosper Mérimée's *Carmen* and Yasmine Ghata's *The Calligraphers' Night*.

SELECTED TITLES FROM HESPERUS PRESS

Brief Lives

Author	Title
Richard Canning	*Brief Lives: Oscar Wilde*
David Carter	*Brief Lives: Honoré de Balzac*
Melissa Valiska Gregory and Melisa Klimaszewski	*Brief Lives: Charles Dickens*
Gavin Griffiths	*Brief Lives: Joseph Conrad*
Patrick Miles	*Brief Lives: Anton Chekhov*
Fiona Stafford	*Brief Lives: Jane Austen*

Classics, Modern Voices and New Fiction

Author	Title	Foreword writer
Honoré de Balzac	*Colonel Chabert*	A.N. Wilson
Honoré de Balzac	*Sarrasine*	Kate Pullinger
Charles Baudelaire	*On Wine and Hashish*	Margaret Drabble
Cyrano de Bergerac	*Journey to the Moon*	Andrew Smith
Alexandre Dumas	*The Corsican Brothers*	Frank Wynne
Gustave Flaubert	*Memoirs of a Madman*	Germaine Greer
Gustave Flaubert	*November*	Nadine Gordimer
Laurent Gaudé	*The Scortas' Sun*	
Yasmine Ghata	*The Calligraphers' Night*	
Joris-Karl Huysmans	*With the Flow*	Simon Callow
Guy de Maupassant	*Butterball*	Germaine Greer
Prosper Mérimée	*Carmen*	Philip Pullman
Antoine François Prévost	*Manon Lescaut*	Germaine Greer
Marcel Proust	*Pleasures and Days*	A.N. Wilson
Marquis de Sade	*Incest*	Janet Street-Porter
Stendhal	*Letters to Pauline*	Adam Thirlwell
Emile Zola	*For a Night of Love*	A.N. Wilson